China

The Business Traveller's Handbook

Gorilla Guides
Travel handbooks for the business jungle

CHINA

First American edition published in 2009 by
INTERLINK TRAVEL
An imprint of Interlink Publishing Group, Inc.
46 Crosby Street
Northampton, Massachusetts 01060
www.interlinkbooks.com

ISBN: 978-1-56656-737-4

Series originator: Max Scott
Series editor: Christopher Ind
Assistant editor: Charles Powell
Design: Nimbus Design
Photography: © Nara Tourism Federation/JNTO
Cartography: Amber Sheers
Printing: Oriental Press, UAE

China

The Business Traveller's Handbook

Navjot Singh

The number of automobiles in China has grown at speed in recent years; however, as these commuters in Guangzhou attest, the bicycle is still a popular form of transport.

Opened in 1996, Beijing's West Station serves destinations to the north and west of the capital.

Hong Kong Central district with the "Two IFC Tower" in the background.

2008 was a very important year for China – the Olympics raising Beijing's profile on the international stage.

The Great Wall, China's premier tourist attraction, stretches over 4,000 miles from Shanhaiguan in the east to Lop Nur in the west.

Hong Kong, seen here from Kowloon across Victoria Harbour, is dazzling in the evening, when skyscrapers light the night sky.

Along the Bund, Shanghai's historic heart, colonial buildings line the western bank of the Huanpu.

Brightly coloured restaurants line Beijing Lu, Guangzhou's popular shopping area.

Acknowledgements

During my years in China, friends, colleagues and others, including people at the British Chamber of Commerce and the American and British Embassies, have provided me with generous advice and support in order for me to collect relevant information. I thank them all. I am also in great debt to my family for putting up with my constant tapping on the computer late at night in order to get this book completed.

Navjot Singh
October 2008

Contents

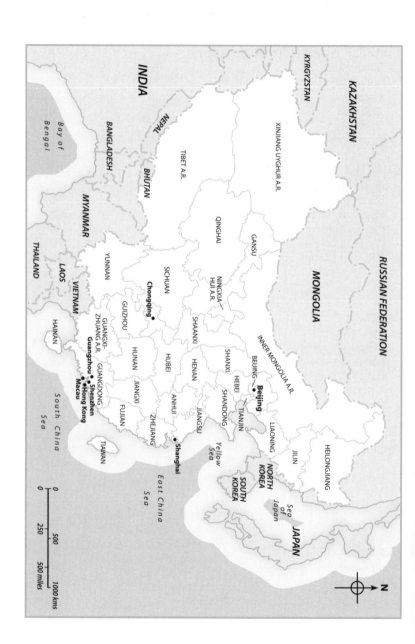

China

1

China yesterday and today

China yesterday and today

A bird's-eye view of the nation,
its history and the special features
that distinguish it from other countries

A condensed history

The modern country

1

Overview of a nation

Over five thousand years of China's history, this great country has developed a civilisation that has endured longer than any other before it. The Chinese name for the country is **'Zhōnghuá Rénmín Gònghéguó'**, however in everyday usage it is referred to as: 'Zhōng Guoó' (meaning 'Middle Kingdom').

The capital is Beijing, or Peking as some still know it. Other major cities of central importance to the emergence of modern China include Guangzhou, Shanghai, Shenzhen, Chongqing, Wuhan, Harbin and Dalian. The country is made up of twenty-two provinces, four special municipalities, five autonomous regions (that include Tibet and Xinjiang Province), and two Special Administrative Regions (SAR). In addition to the five established Special Economic Zones (SEZ), there are also fifteen free-trade zones, thirty-two state-level economic and technological development zones, and an amazing fifty-three new-and high-tech industrial development zones.

The two SARs are Hong Kong, handed over from British rule in 1997, and Macau, which was a Portuguese colony prior to 1999. Although this book will cover China as a whole country, special emphasis will be made to Guangzhou, Shenzhen, Shanghai and of course, Beijing, as these cities form China's major business centres.

Geographically, climatically and culturally diverse, China is a country of rich heritage and immense beauty. As of 2008 figures, China is officially the third largest country by area, covering just over **9,640,821 km²**.

Geography

China's 49 degrees of latitude encompass a climate ranging from subartic to tropical, with altitudes ranging from the peak of Mount Everest, the world's highest mountain (8,847m), to the Turpan Depression at 155m below sea level.

China has a population of just over 1.3 billion people (as of 2007 figures), which is just under 26 per cent of the world's population. Towards the end of 2008, the population of the four major cities in China stood at: Beijing, 18 million, Shanghai, 19 million, Guangzhou, 10 million, and Chongqing, 32 million.

Population

1

There are fifty-six officially recognized ethnic minority groups, plus smaller tribal minorities in rural areas. Approximately ninety-four per cent of the population belongs to the Han identity, while the rest are minority groups made up of: Yao, Zhuang, Hui, Manchu, and She.

Language

The Chinese language has two written forms, traditional and simplified, and the former is used for official documents. The official spoken language is Mandarin (Putonghua), although there are at least sixty-eight various dialects and local languages throughout the country. In southern Chin and Hong Kong, Cantonese (or Guangdonghua) is the dominant dialect, and as such a person from Hong Kong may not be able to understand the spoken Chinese of a person from, say Xian in the north. But they would be able to write and read each others letters or e-mails as the written format is the same throughout the world for all Chinese. This is because the Chinese written characters do not represent sounds or phonetics as western words do. Chinese characters are representative of pictures, with each 'picture' having the same meaning to all Chinese, irrespective of if they are from Taiwan of Singapore. These characters are known as ideographs, because they represent ideas and not names. There are over 55,000 characters in the Chinese language, although only about 3,000 characters are used on a daily basis, and are suffice to read a newspaper or book. (Appendix 2 provides a more detailed look at the language.)

Religion

Banned during the Cultural Revolution, today the official State policy towards religion is tolerance. Although people are permitted to practise religion in their own way, all religions must be registered with the state and people may not encourage or invite others into their religious activities. For these reasons many Chinese keep their religious beliefs a private matter.

Originating in the sixth century BC, the ethical teachings of Confucius (Kong Fuzi) have been very influential in Chinese culture – Confucianism is still widely practised today, along with Buddhism, Taoism, Islam and Christianity.

There are many beautiful Buddhist temples across China as well as Christian Churches (Approximately 16,000 in 2007) and Mosques (Approximately 40,000 in 2007). Although the majority of Chinese people don't believe in god or follow any particular religion, China is home to approximately 102 million Buddhists, approximately nine million Muslims and around fourteen million Christians.

Agriculture has been in the hearts and minds of the Chinese people for hundreds of years – and it was Chairman Mao's belief that farmers should be respected and encouraged as much as possible in order to assist with the growth of the country. Aside from the mountain ranges in the central and western parts of the country (which comprise over a third of the total area) and the deserts of the north, much of the land along the great rivers is immensely fertile. Most agricultural work has been taken over by machines, although in some rural areas, including the tea and rice plantations, traditional methods are still practiced, using hand ploughs and oxen (although this is slowly becoming a vanishing tradition).

Agriculture

China's staple crop is rice (mostly grown in southern and central China) with wheat, barley and millet being widely grown across the north. Soya beans, sugar, cotton and lentils are also abundant throughout the country. Tea is grown on the vast plantations in central, southern and western China.

One of the most abundant and widely grown crops in China is bamboo. It is remarkably strong, and still much used in construction in the cities today.

A brief history of China

China's rich history has been nothing short of a rollercoaster ride, with successions of dynasties rising and falling, bringing progress and in time disintegrating, slowly paving the way for the future of this great country. Like many great civilizations, Chinese history has had its fair share of natural disasters, wars and foreign incursions, yet through it all extraordinary art and literature has been produced, and science has thrived, both in times of war and peace.

1

Ancient History

During the past 2,500 years Chinese civilisation, with its sophisticated administration and advanced culture, has far surpassed most other countries. The Chinese are one of the most proud and hard working people you will ever meet, and with the rising economy, people in this country believe strongly that China is the future. The roots of this hard working culture lie in China's history. Many of the most important inventions and discoveries of the past millennia originated from China. Chinese science, transmitted to Europe, Africa and the Middle East in waves, laid the foundations for many of the constituents of the modern world. Indeed, the Chinese are known worldwide for their work ethic, ingenuity and prolific output; we in the West take many products for granted without noticing that they are in actual fact 'Made in China'. Approximately 3,500 years ago the Chinese were heavily involved in the trade of silk, carving jade (both silk and jade are of high importance to the culture even today) as well as growing wheat and rice.

The first known dynasty was the Xia Dynasty. The Xia ruled from approximately 2000 to 1600 BC. By 1066 BC (at the tail end of the Shang dynasty) a full written language had been developed and the first Chinese calendar introduced. Next came the period of the Western and Eastern Zhou (pronounced Chou) dynasty (1066-221 BC). This period saw the introduction of money, formal laws, metals (including Iron) and the birth of the philosophies of Taoism and Confucianism. Confucianism led to the idea of a 'Mandate of Heaven' (known as Ti'en Ming), in which the Heavens gave the rulers a mandate to impose laws on the people. Ultimately this led to the Chinese addressing their Emperors as the 'Son of Heaven'. This concept has been very much alive in Chinese culture, right up until the death of Chairman Mao Zedong in 1976.

During the period between 481 and 221 BC the Zhou Empire fragmented; this period became known as the 'Warring States Period'. Even today historians refer to the Zhou Empire as the golden age in Chinese history and the Chinese are still very proud of this era as it laid the firm foundations for the China we know today.

1

In 221 BC emperor Qin Shi Huangdi united the individual states into one empire, founding the Qin Dynasty (Pronounced 'Chin'). His tomb, together with some seven thousand terracotta soldiers, a vivid illustration of the armies of the time, was discovered in 1974 in the city of X'ian. The Qin dynasty favoured construction projects over agriculture and began construction of the Great Wall, a monumental man-made structure that stretches over two thousand kilometres, claimed to be visible from space by the naked eye; it has become one of the iconic attractions of China. The consequent famine that resulted from the lack of concentration on agriculture, led to a farmer's revolt, and eventually ended in the fall of the Qin Dynasty.

Qin Dynasty (221-207 BC)

Subsequent to the Qin's ruling, came the four hundred year reign of the Western and Eastern Han dynasties which oversaw the increase of relations with cultures in Central Asia. This allowed China to exchange its silk for precious minerals, such as gold, all along the famous Silk Road that runs through the northwest of China and into some countries in Central Asia.

Han Dynasty (206B.C. till 220AD)

During this period, Buddhism from India was established for the first time in China. Despite the Han Dynasty's administration lasting for only approximately four hundred years, its influence was of vital importance to the Chinese people, and even today the native Chinese are known as the 'Han' people or 'Han Ren' (含人) in Mandarin.

The Han dynasty's demise, bought on by peasant rebellions and Taoist 'Yellow Turbans', plunged the country into four hundred years of civil war that split the country into three territories (Wei, Chu and Wu Dynasties). Eventually the Sui Dynasty came into power, which formed a new government and reunited China.

The Three Kingdoms (220-581) and Sui Dynasty (581-618)

The Sui dynasty gave way to the Tang dynasty. The Tang dynasty had its government seat based in the capital of Shaanxi province, Xian (then known as Chang'An). The Tang dynasty did not last long, as it was brought down by war and economic decline. It was followed by

The Tang Dynasty (618-907)

1

a period of approximately fifty years of no rule until the arrival of the Song dynasty in AD 960.

Song Dynasties (960-1279)

The beginning of the Song dynasty was a time in China's history when trade flourished, especially with Africa and the Middle East. In the last years of the Song dynasty's rule an explorer from the west called Marco Polo arrived in China. His travels in the country lasted almost two decades.

After another period of war, the rulers of the Song Dynasty gave China peace, prosperity and cultural enrichment. Painting and literature were to be found in abundance, along with inventions such as gunpowder, fireworks, paper and porcelain. The Song Dynasty was also the first government to introduce banknotes and paper money. But amidst this growth and prosperity there was a considerable threat looming in northern China.

The Mongol Empire (the Yuan Dynasty, 1279-1368)

Genghis Khan, emperor of the Mongol Empire, which had already taken control of Russia and Central Asia, overthrew China in 1279, thereby ending the rule of the Song dynasty. The grandson of Genghis Khan, Kublai Khan, took control of Beijing and declared the city the capital of the Mongol Empire.

Ming Dynasty (1368-1644)

The Mongols did not last long and were eventually succeeded by the Ming dynasty in 1368. The Ming Dynasty restored rule with its two strong emperors Hongwu and Yongle, who subsequently moved the capital from Nanjing to Beiping (Northern Peace) renaming it Beijing (Northern Capital). It was during the reign of the Ming dynasty that the first foreigners arrived in China by sea; they were the Portuguese and they arrived in the southern city of Guangzhou in 1516. It was around this time that the Portuguese started making Macau a home away from home. The British, Spanish and the Dutch soon followed. The Ming dynasty, instead of focusing on these foreign visitors that were coming into southern China, were distracted by threats from other directions, such as Mongolian highwaymen and Japanese pirates in northern China. Holding off invasions from all sides proved very difficult for the emperors of the Ming Dynasty.

1

With the decline of the Ming Dynasty, China once again found itself under foreign rule. A peasant revolt led to invasion by the Manchus from the north. Under the Manchus, who reunited Manchuria with China, and annexed more territories, the country became isolated from outside influence.

In the early 1840s the British began selling smuggled Indian-grown opium to the Chinese, in return for tea and silk. This smuggling of Opium caused wide spread addiction throughout the country.

In return for the Opium, the British demanded payment in silver. However with finances running short and the opium trade blossoming, the Qing emperors were not able to meet the demands of the British who confiscated all the opium from Guangdong province. This provided a perfect setting for a conflict between the British and the Qing government and resulted in the commencement of the Opium wars. There were two major opium wars, the first between 1839-42 when the British attacked Guangzhou and Nanjing. The Treaty of Nanking (1842) ended the first Opium war and forced the Chinese to open up five ports (including Hong Kong and Shanghai) for trade purposes with Europe in addition to paying reparations. The second opium war started in 1856 and was again the British and the French against the Qing Dynasty; it lasted for four years.

Qing Dynasty (1644-1911)

More recent history

The Manchu Dynasty succeeded in suppressing the internal Taiping Rebellion (1850-64), but from 1860 to 1894 China was subjected to increasing foreign pressure. In 1895 it was defeated in a war with Japan (1894-95) and Formosa (Now known as Taiwan), was lost to the Japanese. The Chinese people began to realise that the only way to resist foreign aggression was by internal reform. The young emperor Ku'ang Hsu and his advisers issued laws from Beijing that sought to modernise China, however the end result was to stimulate the Dowager Empress Tze-his to incite action and retribution. In time, she gained absolute control, and in the process imprisoned the emperor and executed many reformers.

Manchu Dynasty

1

The Boxer Rebellion (1900)

The 'Boxers' or 'Anti-western society of the harmonious fist' (direct translation from their Chinese name) were a fanatical band that pledged to depose and persecute foreigners. They were formed by peasants, starting in Shandong province. They began the 'Boxer Rebellion', which cemented their nationalistic viewpoint that all foreigners should be expelled from China. The bloodbath that followed included the deaths of many foreigners and the destruction of the infrastructure which they brought with them to China, such as churches, ships, train lines and even homes. This did not last long and eventually the boxers were defeated by foreign armed forces. This brought further bad news for the Qing dynasty, which became powerless literally overnight.

Revolution and Republic

In 1908, both the Emperor Ku'ang and the Dowager Empress Tze-His died within a day of each other, and the Emperor's two year old nephew, Pu Yi, came to the throne as Hsuan T'ung. At the same time, as poverty became widespread, a revolution was inevitable. In 1911 Dr Sun Yat-Sen led the revolt which eventually overthrew the Manchu dynasty and led to the creation of the People's Republic of China. Dr Sun Yet Sen (formally known as Sun Zhongshan) was the leader of the National People's Party (known as the Guomindang) who with his revolutionary leadership in 1911 tried to bring democracy to China. He was partly responsible for the overthrow of the Qing dynasty and the expulsion of foreigners from China. Victory was won in 1912 for the revolutionaries and Dr Sun Yet Sen proudly declared the birth of the People's Republic of China. A new flag was introduced and Dr Sun Yet Sen became an overnight hero, known as the father of modern China. Even today, most cities have parks, roads, educational establishments, shopping centres, hospitals and lakes named after him. The city of his birth, Zhongshan in Guangdong province, bears the great man's name.

Rise of the Chinese Communist Party (CCP) and Mao Zedong

The Chinese Communist Party was founded in 1921 by Mao Zedong and his fellow Marxists. In the same year Dr Sun Yet Sen was elected the leader of the National People's Party, the Guomindang. In the years ahead, both the Communist party and the Guomindang Party worked together on many issues ranging from agriculture, which won them the support from the peasants, to the economy. After Dr Sun Yet Sen's death in 1925, his brother-in-law

Chiang Kai-Shek (Jiang Jieshe) took over the nationalist party. Strangely, instead of working together with the communists, Chiang Kai-Shek decided to break with them and there followed a period of civil unrest from 1926 onwards.

In 1934, led by Mao Zedong, almost 81,000 communists fled the nationalists' millitary campaign in the famous 'Long March' that started in southeast China and made its way to the northwest of the country, stretching a distance of over six thousand miles. By the time the marchers had reached Yan'an in Shaanxi province, only eleven per cent of the troops had survived the journey. Coming from an affluent farmer's family, Mao had belief and trust in peasants, miners and labourers.

In 1937 the Japanese took control of Shanghai, moving on to Beijing, Nanjing (where the Nanjing massacre occured) and finally to Guangzhou. These were painful times for the Chinese, who faced terrible Japanese aggression. According to many Chinese history books, bodies, some horribly mutilated by the Japanese Samurai, lay scattered in the major cities Shanghai and Nanjing and people were starving to death. Even today many Chinese still harbour ill feelings towards the Japanese for this period. Although with time relations between the two nations are improving, as evidenced by the fact that many Chinese people today drive Japanese cars and indulge in Japanese food.

During the Second World War the Japanese again attacked major northern cities, especially Shanghai, where many foreigners were trapped by the unfortunate events. After the Japanese finally surrendered to allied forces in 1945, a civil war erupted between the Nationalists and the Communists, and in 1949 the Red Army (later known as the People's Liberation Army or PLA) led by the great Mao Zedong defeated the Nationalists in Nanjing. Chiang Kai-Shek withdrew to Taiwan (then known as Formosa Island) along with two million other refugees.

The victorious Chinese Communist Party led by Mao himself, declared the People's Republic of China on

1

1 October 1949 in the great Tiananmen Square in front of millions of people.

Subsequent to the declaration of the People's Republic, China in the early 1950s seemed to be prospering. Then, with the economy improving, Mao Zedong introduced the ambitious and infamous 'Great leap forward' in 1958, a five year grand plan to accelerate the Chinese economy in a kind of 'fast track scheme' to put it on a par with most developed countries. Unfortunately, this did not succeed as the communist party had hoped, partly as a result of natural disasters which caused widespread damage to the economy in 1960-61. During this time China sadly bore the brunt of the world's worst famine which led to the deaths of between fourteen and forty million people.

China's economy spiralled down bringing about massive protests from students in 1966, who denounced the administration of their educational establishments. This brought upon an era that Chairman Mao echoed as the 'Great Cultural Revolution'. Under Mao's teachings, many of Beijing's students organised themselves into a political private army called the 'Red Guards'.

During this period China was effectively separated from the world as all western philosophies were neglected. Mao consistently encouraged the Chinese people to emulate the farmers and the poor. His famous slogan 'the poorer the better' was something that people looked up to during the Cultural Revolution. China, in those days, was in a state of chaos that led to academics being publicly humiliated and tortured.

Chairman Mao died on 9 September 1976. His portrait is placed on the top of the main gateway of the Forbidden City facing Tiananmen Square in Beijing, where his body is on public display at the mausoleum.

Deng Xiaoping
and the dawn
of modern China

Towards the end of the Cultural Revolution, Deng Xiaoping took control of daily duties within the communist party starting in 1977, and later became the President. With Deng Xiaoping taking the helm, the future looked brighter. Deng actively encouraged foreign trade and, between 1980 and 1984, opened five Special

Economic Zones (SEZ) across the east coast of the country, including the cities of Shenzhen and Shantou, where an open door policy was inaugurated. In contrast to Chairman Mao's slogan of 'the poorer the better', Deng's slogan, 'to get rich is glorious' is certainly being put to good practice in the current climate. Economic and political ties started to improve with the world; a prime example of this was the China-Russia summit in Beijing in May of 1989, the first such summit since 1959. Foreign investment increased and China's economy since 1979 has been doubling every eight years.

Since November 2002, President Hu Jintao has held the position of General Secretary of the Chinese Communist Party. Hu Jintao was elected the President of the People's Republic of China on 15 March 2003 and, in October 2007, re-elected by the National People's Congress in accordance with Article 62 of the 1982 Constitution. Wen Jiabao has been the Premier of the State Council of the People's Republic of China since March 2003.

Hong Kong was a British Colony from 1842 until 1997 when it was handed over to the People's Republic of China. Its official name is now Hong Kong Special Administrative Region (HK SAR).

Hong Kong SAR

The first governor of Hong Kong was Sir Charles Elliot, who declared himself the governor of Britain's colonial acquisition in the Far East in 1841 whilst on board the HMS Wellesley, which was moored just off Hong Kong Island. The same day, January 26, Captain Edward Belcher of the Royal Navy raised the Union Jack on Hong Kong. This was the beginning of the long complicated history of the Hong Kong we know today.

The last British governor of Hong Kong was Chris Patten, who endeavoured to extend the democracy enjoyed in the Colony into mainland China before the handover. Even today Hong Kong retains a degree of free speech and feeling of 'openness' that one may not experience on the mainland. Most of the diplomatic and political events that led to the handover of Hong Kong to the Chinese are covered well in Patten's book *Not Quite the Diplomat*, which was published in September 2005.

The title 'Governor' of Hong Kong was replaced with the title of 'Chief Executive' after the 1997 handover. The current Chief Executive of Hong Kong is Sir Donald Tsang Yam-Kuen (More commonly known as Donald Tsang), who has held the position since 25 June 2005, and was re-elected, for a second and final term from 2007 to 2012, on 25 March 2007 in a contested small-circle election.

As you cross the border from Hong Kong back to Shenzhen, the environmental change is quite dramatic and can be a bit of a shock to anyone coming to China for the first time – it really does feel as if you have stepped thirty years back in time (or forward if you are going to Hong Kong from the mainland). Since independence from the British in 1997, Hong Kong has still managed to retain many of the traditions that are forbidden in mainland China. Speaking English in Hong Kong is not a problem as it used to be a British Colony. Cantonese is the traditional language of Hong Kong and not many people understand Mandarin.

The majority of British expats left following the handover in 1997, however there are still a considerable number who have decided to keep Hong Kong their second home. Most British subjects are employed in the financial and insurance sectors (many Investment Banks have their Asia Pacific headquarters in Hong Kong).

Macau SAR

Macau lies on the border of Guangdong Province's southernmost city, Zhuhai, and was, until 1999, a Portuguese colony. The Portuguese left their own legacies in Macau. The language remains as almost every sign is both in Mandarin and Portuguese. The currency used here is the 'Patacas'. There are two islands, Taipa and Coloane, connected to the main territory by a bridge and a causeway. Founded by the Portuguese in 1557, Macau declined as a regional trading centre in the early 19th century with the rise of Hong Kong, which had the advantage of being a deep water port.

Initial negotiations for the handover of Macau back to the Chinese began in the 1980s and, in 1987, an agreement was reached by both governments to hand over Macau in 1999. The country was then declared a Special Administrative Region (SAR). Just like Hong Kong, Macau is governed under the One country- two systems approach and has a Chief Executive who manages the day to day running of the SAR. Macau has not quite hit the international scene as Hong Kong has, however it has quietly been establishing itself as the 'Las Vegas' of Asia because of the large number of Casinos being built.

6000-4000 BC	Archaeological evidence of fishing and farming in Southern China.
2000-1500 BC	Xia Dynasty
1500-1066 BC	Shang Dynasty
1066-221 BC	Zhou Dynasty
221-206	First Emperor of China, Qin Shi Huangdi, unites the country and gives China it's name. The Great Wall of China begun.
206-220 AD	Han Dynasty
250-581	The Three Kingdoms
581-618	Sui Dynasty
618-907	Tang Dynasty
960-1279	Song Dynasties
1279-1368	Mongols invade China and form the Yuan Dynasty. Genghis Khan conquers northern China and his grandson Kublai Khan becomes Mongol emperor of the whole of China.
1368-1644	Ming Dynasty
1516	Portuguese arrive in Guangdong Province
1644-1911	Qing Dynasty – China ruled by the Manchus of Manchuria
1839-42	First Opium War
1841	British arrive in Hong Kong and Admiral Charles Elliot declares himself Governor from onboard HMS Wellesley.
1842	Treaty of Nanking (Nanjing) ends first Opium war. Chinese ports forced to open to foreign trade and Hong Kong ceded to Britain.
1843	Hong Kong formally declared a British Crown Colony.
1864	Hong Kong and Shanghai Bank (HSBC) founded.

Notable Events
in China's Past

1

1888	Funicular tramway to the Peak on Hong Kong Island Is built.
1898	Britain extracts a further concession with a 99-year lease on the New Territories to end on 1 July 1997.
1900	The Boxer Rebellion sparked by concessions gained by foreign powers.
1908	Dowager Empress Tze-Hsi passes away. Child Pu Yi is proclaimed the Emperor Hsuan T'ung.
1912	Revolution removes the Child Emperor.
	Republic of China is proclaimed. Dr Sun Yat-Sen becomes first Provisional president of China before Mao Zedong.
1921	Chinese Communist Party (CCP) is founded.
1923-31	First United Front between CCP and the Guomindang Nationalist Party.
1934-35	CCP forces retreat from the Guomindang in the Long March. 10,000 out of the 100,000 survive the 6,000 mile journey.
1937	Japan invades China, with Shanghai taking the brunt of the damage. Second front between the Guomindang and the CCP.
1945	Second World War ends with the defeat of Japan by the Allies.
1949	People's Liberation Army (PLA) takes over Shanghai.
	People's Republic of China (PRC) founded by Mao Zedong who is elected Chairman. Nationalists withdraw to Taiwan (Known then as Formosa)
1958-61	The 'Great Leap Forward' results in famine that kills over thirty million Chinese people.
1976	Mao Zedong and Premier Zhou Enlai pass away.
1993	Jiang Zemin appointed President of China
1997	Deng Xiaoping passes away. Hong Kong returns to China. System of one government and two systems is put in place.
1999	Macau handed back to China by the Portuguese.
2001	On July 13 2001, the IOC awarded Beijing to host the 2008 Olympic games.
2002	President Hu Jintao replaces Jiang Zemin.

| 2007 | President Hu Jintao elected by the party as President for his second and possibly last term until 2012. |
| 2008 | Beijing hosts the Olympic Games, opening on the eighth day of the eighth month. |

China today

A visitor to London or New York after a twenty-year absence would probably not see a dramatic difference. Almost any major city in China, by contrast, would be all but unrecognisable.

Today still a communist country, remarkably communism in China goes hand in hand with consumerism and the traditional Chinese way of life. China manages to combine these better than any other country has done in history. Cities like Beijing, Guangzhou and Chongqing are growing at a phenomenal pace, while keeping their traditional and historical customs and monuments largely intact.

Some economists are confident that China's economy is set to overtake that of the United States and Japan by 2050. In 2008, China's economy was already the fourth largest in the world.

The current Chinese government has in recent years made a number of attempts to sustain friendships with neighbouring countries as well as form new friendships with countries that, in the past, China has had differences with. There has been interest in building a stronger partnership with other emerging markets such as India, Korea and many countries in the African continent. Ever since the formation of the Communist Party in 1921, there have been strong relations with Russia as well as with all the major European countries. Germany, France, Italy, Australia, Pakistan and the USA are among some of China's many trading partners. China has enjoyed membership to the UN Security Council since November 1971. Economic think-tanks often point out that no country in this day and age can afford to make enemies with China because it is the place to be in the future.

1

Relationships with neighbouring countries, including India and Japan, have improved in recent years. The former was at war with China in 1962 over a border dispute, but since the early part of the millennium, there have been many displays of friendship between these two Asian giants. The world's attention these days is, of course, on India and China. Both countries have in common large diverse populations, booming and steadily rising economic rates (which have been maintained at double figures for the past few years), and a growing number of educated young people who are contributing to the futures of their countries. Both countries have become a haven for multinationals looking to out-source their facilities to manufacturing plants set up in India and China.

Making friends around the world

China and India declared friendship years in 2006 and 2007 respectively, which saw many joint activities such as trade fairs promoting each other's businesses, and even joint military exercises (war games) – this is amazing considering the fact that they were arch enemies for quite a number of years.

The friendship between China and many African countries has continued to become stronger each year over the past decade. China has invested heavily in assisting African countries to improve their infrastructure, economy and healthcare. In the Africa-China summit in Beijing in 2006, President Hu Jintao promised more than $5 billion in support for Africa in the next five years, to be spent on vital infrastructure such as bridges, buildings, homes, hospitals and much needed medical facilities for rural areas.

Many African countries that have been deprived as a result of war or famine, or other unfortunate causes, have been making progress towards a better future thanks in part to China's efforts. China has provided numerous professionals for many African countries in recent years, such as Doctors, Engineers and Nurses. There is more information on the China-Africa Business council website: www.cabc.org.cn.

Since the inaugural service of the Qinghai to Lhasa train route in the summer of 2006 'the world's highest railway', Tibet has become more open to the world, both as an economic region and a tourist destination. Some of the restrictions that have been in place in the past may eventually be lifted, giving way to the millions of tourists and business people who want to establish a presence in Tibet.

In October 2007 the 17th Party Congress, which is the highest state body and only legislative house in the People's Republic of China, announced the selection of the following nine members (listed in order of official ranking):

Hu Jintao:	President of the People's Republic of China, General Secretary of the Communist Party of China and Chairman of the Central Military Commission
Wu Bangguo:	Chairman of the Standing Committee of the National People's Congress.
Wen Jiabao:	Premier of the State Council of the People's Republic of China.
Jia Qinglin:	Chairman of the National Committee of the Chinese People's Political Consultative Conference
Li Changchu:	Head of the CPC CC – Former Guangdong Party Secretary
Xi Jinping:	High-ranking member of CPC Secretariat
Li Keqiang	No official position assigned or revealed
He Guoqiang:	Head of Central Commission for Discipline Inspection
Zhou Yongkang:	Head of Political and Legislative Affairs Committee

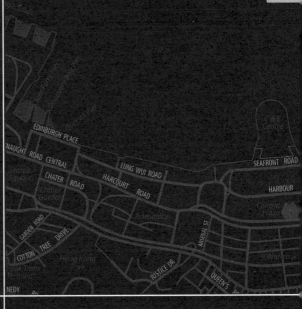

2

investigating the potential market

investigating the potential market

An outline of some of the myriad organisations which exist to assist the exporter, along with an assessment of their focus and likely relevance

2

Overview

The business traveller should endeavour to be as well informed as possible before entering the China market. China provides many challenges, but if these are approached correctly then, of course, your business can be extremely successful. There is a wide range of advice provided by chambers of commerce, embassies, your country's trade and industry organisation, expatriate websites as well as sound advice from other corporate professionals who have lived and worked in China. In addition to the usual problems that come with setting up a business in a foreign country, what set China apart from other markets are the challenges of language, culture, regulation and legalisation.

The central concerns of western businesses making strategic decisions in China is obtaining accurate market information. James AC Sinclair, senior consultant at InterChina Consulting in Shanghai comments in his report 'Market Information Paradox':

Market information

'China is an enormous, complex and dynamic market. In the West, the market information structure is such that businesses have often been operating in their markets long enough to have developed a strong understanding of their markets. In contrast, the market information structure in China is relatively weak. Many western businesses are new to their markets in China, and for almost all the first impression is one of opaqueness rather than transparency. Western businesses can't just turn to their investment bank analysts, as the view from the ivory towers in Shanghai looks quite different from the reality on the ground in say, Sichuan for example.'

It is important that the information that you get is accurate and genuine. Foreign companies have complained of falling prey to foreign management consultants in China who are basically professional conmen, providing inaccurate or limited information in return for overpriced consultation fees. If you are suspicious, usually the best way is to get in touch with their company's Head Office in Europe or North America to make sure that you are dealing with the right person in China.

From my experience, we invited a 'Management Consultant' who charged our corporation in Shenzhen 15,000RMB (Approx $1900USD) for a single day's consultation, which our senior management had suspicions about when people started leaving in the middle of meetings because the advice he was providing was not as professional as one would have expected from someone charging those rates. After an initial investigation with the company HQ in London, we were glad to hear he was released from his China position the following week.

Chambers of commerce

Below is a list of all the Chambers of commerce which have a presence in China. Contact details for the Beijing branch, which is usually the Headquarters for most countries' Chamber's offices, is provided (unless otherwise stated). The list also contains the China Head Office address of the European Chamber of Commerce in China (EUCCC). Formed with the assistance of the EU Delegation in Beijing on 19th October 2000, it is a non-profit membership fee-based organization. The EUCCC has seven offices throughout mainland China aimed at developing bilateral agreements and cooperation between EU Member states and China.

EUCCC

Canada, Australia, America, India, Singapore, as well as various EU countries have strong trade and personal relationships with China. With some countries this relationship is built on the fact that many natives of China and Hong Kong have set up businesses in countries such as Canada (Vancouver and Toronto), Australia and most recently in India. These countries' respective Chambers of commerce and embassies would be the first point of contact for companies and individuals who want to establish any form of firm business plan in China. If the respective Chamber of commerce or embassy cannot assist then they would be in a position to point you in the right direction. Most of the information is free of charge, although some specialised advice may include a small fee. For this it is best to investigate and judge for yourself which is the best option for your business.

2

Contact details of other branches in China for the relevant Chamber of commerce may be obtained from their HQ office as listed below:

American Chamber of Commerce
China Resource Building, Suite 1903
8 Jianguomenbei Ave
Beijing 100005, PRC
Tel: +86 (0)10 8519 1920
Fax: +86 (0)10 8519 1910
Email: amcham@amcham-china.org.cn
Website: www.amcham-china.org.cn

Australian Chamber of Commerce
E floor, Office Tower
Beijing Hong Kong Macau Centre (Swissotel),
2 Chaoyangmenbei Dajie
Beijing, 100027, P. R. China
Tel: +86 (0)10 6595 9252
Fax: +86 (0)10 6595 9253
E-mail: info@austcham.org
Website: www.austcham.org

Austrian Chamber of Commerce in Hong Kong
GPO Box 8031
Central, Hong Kong
Tel: +852 3105 0152
Fax: +852 3105 9925
Email: austrocham@austrocham.com
Website: www.aa.com.hk

Belgium Chamber of Commerce
4020 Xinhe Dasha
Sanyuanli
14, Shunyuan Street
Chaoyang District
Beijing, 100027
Tel: + 86 (0)10 6465 0320
Fax: +86 (0)10 6465 2080
Email: beijing@bencham.org
Website: www.bencham.org

2

British Chamber of Commerce
The British Centre
Room 1001
China Life Tower
16 Chaoyangmenwai Avenue
Beijing 100020 China
Tel: +86 (0)10 85251111
Fax: +86 (0)10 85251100
E-mail: britcham@pek.britcham.org
Website: http://www.pek.britcham.org/

Canada China Business Council
Suite 18-2, CITIC Building,
19 Jianguomenwai Street
Beijing, PR China,100004
Tel: +86 (0)10 8526 1820/21/22
Fax: +86 (0)10 6512 6125
E-mail: ccbcbj@ccbc.com.cn
Website: www.ccbc.com

China Council for the Promotion of International Trade (CCPIT)
China Chamber of International Commerce (CCOIC)
1 Fuxingmenwai Street
Beijing 100860, China
Tel: +86 (0)10 88075716
Fax: +86 (0)10 68030747
Website: http://english.ccpit.org/

Danish Chamber of Commerce
Office C412
Beijing Lufthansa Centre
50 Liangmaqiao Road
Chaoyang District
Beijing 100016
Tel: +86 (0)10 6467 5748
Fax: +86 (0)10 6462 3206
E-mail: cathy@dccc.com.cn
Website: www.dccc.com.cn

European Chamber of Commerce
Lufthansa Center, Office S-123
50 Liangmaqiao Road,
Chaoyang District
Beijing 100016, China
Tel: +86 (0)10 6462 2065/66
Fax: +86 (0)10 6462 2067
E-mail: euccc@euccc.com.cn
Website: www.europeanchamber.com.cn

Delegation of the European Commission in China
15, Dong Zhi Men Wai Da Jie
San Li Tun, Beijing 100600
Tel: +86 (0)10 84548000
Fax: +86 (0)10 84548011
E-mail: Delegation-China@ec.europa.eu
Website: http://www.delchn.cec.eu.int/

Economic Representation of Flanders in China
San Li Tun Lu, 6
CN-100600 Beijing
Tel.:   +86 (0)10 6532 4964
Fax: +86 (0)10 6532 6833
E-mail: beijing@fitagency.com

Economic Representation of Wallonia Region in China
San Li Tun Lu, 6
CN-100600 Beijing
Tel.:   +86 (0)10 6532 6695
Fax: +86 (0)10 6532 6696
E-mail: awexbrubeijing@188.com

French Chamber of Commerce
Novotel Xinqiao Beijing
Area B, 6th Floor
2 Dongjiaominxiang
Dongcheng District
Beijing 100004
Tel: +86 (0)10 65 12 17 40
Fax: +86 (0)10 65 12 14 96
E-Mail: ccifc-beijing@ccifc.org
Website: www.ccifc.org

2

Delegation of German Industry & Commerce (AHK)
German Industry & Commerce Beijing Branch (GIC)
Landmark Tower 2, Unit 0811
8 North Dongsanhuan Road
Chaoyang District
100004 Beijing, CHINA
Tel.:   +86 (0)10 65900926 (AHK)
Fax: +86 (0)10 65906313 (AHK)
Tel.:   +86 (0)10 65906151 (GIC)
Fax: +86 (0)10 65906313 (GIC)
Email: info@bj.china.ahk.de
Website: http://china.ahk.de/home/

Italian Chamber of Commerce
Unit 2606-2607, Full Tower
9, Dong San Huan Zhong Lu
Chaoyang District, Beijing
100020
Tel: +86 (0)10 85910545
Fax: +86 (0)10 85910546
E-mail: info@cameraitacina.com
Website: http://cameraitacina.com/

Korea Trade Promotion Corporation (Guangzhou)
Suite 1010-11
Main Tower
Guangdong International Hotel
339 Huanshi-dong Rd.
Guangzhou, 510098
Tel: +86 (0)20 8334 0052,
          +86 (0)20 8334 0170
Fax: +86 (0)20 8335 1142

New Zealand Development Association (Guangzhou)
C950 Office Tower China Hotel
Liu Hua Road
Guangzhou, 510015
Tel: +86 (0)20 8667 0253
Fax: +86 (0)20 8666 6420

Singapore Chamber of Commerce
6th Floor, Office Building
Hong Kong Macau Center
2 Chaoyangmen Bei Dajie
Beijing 100027

People's Republic of China
Tel: +86 (0)10 65539786, 65014242, 65532288
          ext 2143
Fax: +86 (0)10 65011518
Email: singcham@singcham.com.cn
Website: www.singcham.com.cn

Spanish Chamber of Commerce
Room 304B, Great Rock Plaza
13 Xin Zhong Xi Li
Dongcheng District, Beijing
100027, PR China
Tel.:   +86(0)10 6416 9774/7323
Fax: +86(0)10 6416 1534
E-mail: info@spanishchamber-ch.com

Swedish Chamber of Commerce
Room 313, Radisson SAS Hotel
(Beijing Huang Jia Da Fan Dian)
6A, East Beisanhuan Road
Chaoyang District
Beijing 100028
Tel: +86 (0)10 5922 3388 ext. 313
Fax: +86 (0)10 6462 7454
Website: www.swedishchamber.com.cn
E-mail: beijing@swedishchamber.com.cn

Swiss Chamber of Commerce
Suite 100, CIS Tower
38 Liangmaqiao Lu
Chaoyang District
Beijing 100016, China
Tel: +86 (0)10) 6432 2020
Fax: +86 (0)10 6432 3030
E-mail: info@bei.swisscham.org
Website: www.swisscham.org

US-CHINA Business Council
CITIC Building, Suite 10-01
19 Jianguomenwai Dajie
Beijing 100004, China
Tel: +86 (0)10 6592 0727
Fax: +86 (0)10 6512 5854
E-mail: info@uschina.org.cn
Website: www.uschina.org

China-Britain Business Council (CBBC)

The CBBC, with its Head Office in London, is the UK's leading not-for-profit organisation, funded by the UK Trade & Investment (previously known as UK Trade Partners), that provides comprehensive business advice to British companies and individuals doing business in or with China. The CBBC has nine well established offices throughout the major cities in China, as well as four offices in the UK. Whether you are setting up operations in China for the first time or an experienced and established company that already has a presence in China but would like to keep in touch with updates on market developments, the CBBC has a portfolio of experienced professionals who are dedicated to those needs of the business. Over one third of CBBC members are Small to Medium Sized Enterprises (SMEs).

CBBC

The CBBC is a paid membership organization with an annual fee. Membership entitles you to six day's free business support in China, free use of the CBBC library as well as invitations to networking events where you can meet like minded individuals for business prospects and share your views. For companies serious about developing business in China, CBBC membership provides a cost-effective route to on-going support, networking and exclusive services and discounts as listed above.

China-Britain Business Council (Head Office)
1 Warwick Row
London SW1E 5ER
Tel: +44 (0)20 7802 2000
Fax: +44 (0)20 7802 2029
Email: enquiries@cbbc.org
Corporate website: www.cbbc.org

China-Britain Business Council (CBBC)
The British Centre
Room 1001, China Life Tower
16 Chaoyangmenwai Avenue
Beijing 100020
People's Republic of China
Tel: +86 (0)10 8525 1111

Fax: +86 (0)10 8525 1001
Email: beijing@cbbc.org.cn

China-Britain Business Council in Shanghai
Unit 1701-2, Westgate Tower
1038 Nanjing Road W
Shanghai 200041
Peoples Republic of China
Tel: +86 (0)21 6218 5183
Fax: +86 (0)21 6218 5193
Email: shanghai@cbbc.org.cn

China-Britain Business Council in Shenzhen
Room1121, Tower A, International Chamber
of Commerce
Fuhua Yi Lu, Futian District
Shenzhen, 518048, China
Tel: +86 (0)755 8219 8148
Fax: +86 (0)755 8219 3159
Email: shenzhen@cbbc.org.cn

CBI (Confederation of Business Industry)

The CBI is a lobbying organisation for UK business on national and international issues. The CBI works closely with the UK government, international legislators and policy-makers to help UK businesses compete effectively.

CBI policy is decided by their members, most of whom are senior corporate executives from all sectors and sizes of business. There are offices all over the UK, as well as in Beijing (opened 2006), Brussels and Washington.

CBI China Office
1006B, China Life Tower
16 Chaoyangmenwai Ave
Beijing 10002, CHINA
Tel: +86 (0)10 8525 3100
Fax: +86 (0)10 85253 116]
Website: www.cbi.org.uk

CBI

2

CBI Head Office
London Region
Centre Point
103 New Oxford Street
London
WC1A 1DU
Tel: +44 (0)20 7395 8195.
Fax: +44 (0)20 7379 0945
Website: www.cbi.org.uk

Embassies

Here is a list of some Embassies in Beijing. A comprehensive list for all the Embassies and Consulates-General in China for your country may be available from your local government office in your country.

Embassies

Embassy of Australia
21 Dong Zhi Men Wai Da Jie
San Li Tun, Beijing, China
Tel: +86 (0)10 6532 2331
Fax: +86 (0)10 6532 4349
E-mail: pubaff.beijing@dfat.gov.au
Austrade (Commercial Office)
Tel: +86 (0)10 6532 6726 and
          +86 (0)10 6532 6731
Website: www.austemb.org.cn

Embassy of Canada
19, Dong Zhi Men Wai Da Jie
Beijing, China
Tel: +86 (0)10 6532 3536/3031
Fax: +86 (0)10 6532 4072/ 4311
E-mail: bejing@international.gc.ca
Website: www.beijing.gc.ca

Embassy of the Republic of France
3 Dong San Jie, San Li Tun
Beijing, China
Tel: +86 (0)10 6532 1331
Fax: +86 (0)10 6532 4841
Commerical Office: +86 (0)10 6501 4866/ 4870
Website: www.ambafrance-cn.org

2

Embassy of the Federal Republic of Germany
17, Dong Zhi Men Wai Da Jie
Chaoyang District, Beijing, China
Tel: +86 (0)10 85329000
Fax: +86 (0)10 65325336
E-mail: embassy@peki.diplo.de
Commercial Office: +86 (0)10 6532 5556/5560

**Embassy of the United Kingdom of Great Britain
and Northern Ireland**
11, Guang Hua Lu
Beijing, China
Tel: +86 (0)10 51924000
Fax: +86 (0)10 6532 1937
E-mail: commercialmail@peking.mail.fco.gov.uk
Website: http://www.uk.cn/
Foreign & Commonwealth Office (Travel advice etc):
www.fco.gov.uk

Embassy of the United States of America
3, Xiu Shui Bei Jie, Jian Guo Men Wai
Beijing, China
Tel: +86 (0)10 6532 3831
            and +86 (0)10 6532 3431
E-mail: AmCitBeijing@state.gov
Website: http://beijing.usembassy-china.org.cn
US State Government website (for travel advice etc.):
www.state.gov

Other government organisations
UK Trade & Investment

Whether you want to export from the UK to China or
you are a company that wants to invest in the UK, then
UK Trade & Investment would be the first place for you
to approach with your business plan. Originally known
as UK Trade Partners, UK Trade & Investment is an
international organisation with headquarters in London
and Glasgow. The British government has taken trade
activities with China quite seriously in recent years.
When you read that in 2007, only roughly 1 per cent
of UK trade was with China, and while the UK imports
just over US$11 billion of Chinese goods every year, it
only exports approximately US$2 billion of goods to
China, it does make you wonder why foreign

UK Trade and
Investment

2

governments have only recently started cooperating with China. Working alongside UK Embassies, High Commissions and trade offices in China, UK Trade & Investment can assist UK businesses to settle in China or assist China based businesses to locate to the UK. UK Trade & Investment brings together the work of the Foreign & Commonwealth Office (FCO) and the Department for Business, Enterprise and Regulatory Reform into one organisation.

Contact details for the UK Trade & Investment are as follows:

UK Trade & Investment London International Trade Team
New City Court
20 St. Thomas Street
London SE1 9RS
Tel: 0207 234 3000
Fax: 0207 234 3001
Website: www.uktradeinvest.gov.uk

UK Trade & Investment has four offices in China, based at the Embassy and Consulates-General in Beijing, Shanghai, Guangzhou and Chongqing. The contact details for the British Embassy are given earlier in this chapter, from there they can advise you on other contact details within China. Further information will be provided by your Chamber of Commerce in China (list provided above).

Hong Kong Trade Development Council

HKTDC

The HKTDC is the main body responsible for the promotion of trade between Hong Kong and other countries. With its Head Office in Hong Kong, as well a global network of 41 offices on five continents, the HKTDC can assist foreign companies that want to establish business in Hong Kong. HKDTC's global body, the Federation of Hong Kong Business Associations Worldwide (www.hkfederation.org.hk) has a network of 31 Hong Kong business associations in 23 countries and regions. HKDTC have dedicated professionals that are the first port of call for overseas and mainland businesses looking for Hong Kong suppliers, buyers or partners. The

HKTDC also assists Hong Kong Business Associations around the world with over 10,000 members who are mostly within the SME market with special partnership ties to Hong Kong. In addition to Internet services, HKDTC also publishes useful trade directories and products/services magazines. With over a million online subscribers and over two million global subscribers to their publications, HKDTC have made a solid impression on the global business market, and make business sourcing easier for international buyers.

HKDTC Head Office
38/F, Office Tower, Convention Plaza
1 Harbour Road, Wanchai,
Hong Kong
Tel: +852 2584 4333
Fax: +852 2824 0249
E-mail: hktdc@tdc.org.hk
Corporate Website: www.tdctrade.com

London Office
16 Upper Grosvenor Street
London W1K 7PL
England
Tel: +44 (0)207 616 9500
Fax: +44 (0)207 616 9510
E-mail: london.office@tdc.org.hk
Website: http://uk.tdctrade.com/

New York Office
219 East 46th Street
New York, NY 10017
USA
Tel: +1 212 838 8688
Fax: +1 212 838 8941
E-mail: new.york.office@tdc.org.hk

India-China Trade Link

The 21st century's global attention is firmly focused on the respective lands of the Elephant and the Dragon. Both these countries have a lot to offer with their large educated workforce, and are firmly in a position to assist western economies set trade relationships with them. **The India-China Trade Link** (www.ficci-ccpit.com)

Trade relationships

2

is an organisation that is made up of the **FICCI (Federation of Indian Chamber of Commerce & Industry)** and the **CCPIT (China Council for the Promotion of International Trade)**.

FICCI India Office
Federation House
Tansen Marg
New Delhi, 110001
Tel.:   +91 (0)11 23738760-70
Fax: +91 (0)11 23721504, 23320714
E-mail: ficci@ficci.com
Website: www.ficci.com

FICCI China Office
U-Space Building
A-1701, Guangqumenwai Street
Chaoyang District
Beijing - 100022
China
Tel: +86 (0)10 5861 2342/5861 2344
Fax: +86 (0)10 5861 3409
Email: ficci@ficci.com

China Council for the Promotion of International Trade (CCPIT)
China Chamber of International Commerce (CCOIC)
1 Fuxingmenwai Street
Beijing 100860, P.R.China
Tel: +86 (0)10 88075716
Fax: +86 (0)10 68030747
Website: www.ccpit.org

Other foreign trade organisations
Australian Government department of Foreign Affairs & Trade
R.G. Casey Building,
John McEwen Crescent,
Barton, ACT, 0221 Australia
Website: www.dfat.gov.au

Foreign Affairs and International Trade Canada
125 Sussex Drive
Ottawa, ON, Canada
K1A 0G2
Tel: +1 613 944 4000
Website: www.international.gc.ca

It may also be worthwhile reading the relevant
material on the following Chinese government
website. All websites are in English and Chinese.

China Ministry of Commerce
www.mofcom.gov.cn

State Economic & Trade Commission
www.setc.gov.cn

State Food and Drug Administration
www.sfda.gov.cn

Certification and Accreditation Administration
www.cnca.gov.cn

Standardization Administration of China
www.sac.gov.cn

Chinese Academy of Sciences
www.cas.cn

Ministry of Foreign Affairs
www.fmprc.gov.cn

National Bureau of Statistics of China
www.stats.gov.cn

Development Research Centre of the State Council
www.drc.gov.cn

Chinese Academy of Engineering
www.cae.cn

China National Light Industry
www.clii.com.cn

2

China Machinery Industry Federation
www.mei.gov.cn

Invest in China & Invest Hong Kong

CIPA

Invest in China is an organization that was set up by China's government as a Investment Promotion Agency of the Ministry of Commerce (CIPA). The CIPA is engaged in Chinese investment promotion processes and is in charge of 'Inviting in', through the FDI in China (address listed below), and 'Going global' (outbound investment). Its two-way investment promotion is similar to that of the UK Trade & Investment organisation.

Invest in China

Rm A717 Century Plaza
No.99 Wangfujing street,
Dongcheng district, Beijing
100006, P.R. of China
Tel: +86 (0)10 65287383 /85226521
Fax: +86 (0)10)65287362/85226521
E-mail: service@fdi.gov.cn
Website: www.fdi.gov.cn

Invest Hong Kong is a Government support organisation, whose purpose is to provide funding support schemes and programmes, as well as infrastructure support to businesses that are considering entering into the Hong Kong market. For many new comers who want to establish a business in China, the best way is to start in Hong Kong and then make in roads in the mainland.

Invest Hong Kong

15/F, One Pacific Place
Queensway,
Hong Kong
Tel: +852 3107 1000
Fax: +852 3107 9007
E-mail: enq@InvestHK.gov.hk
Website: www.investhk.gov.hk

Credit Guarantees

Export Credits Guarantee Department (ECGD)

This is a government department that reports to the Minister for Trade and Industry in the UK. It is the UK's official export credit agency. ECGD helps by working closely with exporters, project sponsors, banks and buyers to win business and complete overseas contracts by putting together the right package for each contract and assisting them with capital equipment and project-related goods and services. If a borrower fails to repay any part of the loan, the UK bank is covered by the ECGD guarantee.

Among other services, they also provide Insurance to UK exporters against non-payment by their overseas buyers and guarantees for bank loans to facilitate the provision of finance to buyers of goods and services from UK companies.

ECGD
PO Box 2200
2 Exchange Tower
Harbour Exchange Square
London E14 9GS
Tel: +44 (0)20 7512 7000
Fax: +44 (0)20 7512 7649
Email: Help@ecgd.gsi.gov.uk

Export.gov

This is the official US government export portal that assists American businesses that want to export to China or vice-versa. It is called the China Business Information Center (China BIC) and their website contains a range of useful information on establishing good links with businesses in China or setting up business in China. The website also has links to useful issues such as intellectual property (IP), law and trade shows in the major cities in China.
Website: http://www.export.gov/china/
Website: http://www.buyusa.gov/china/en/

2

ECGD

China BIC

2

Management consultancies that provide advice to foreign companies in China

For many large corporations, getting some sound advice from international management consultancies is the best possible way to research and investigate the Chinese market before setting foot there. Unlike other countries, in Europe for example, where corporations can go and buy land and then set up a business within a couple of months (if not weeks), in China there are myriad issues which newcomers have to take into account. These are not limited to culture and language; one must also bear in mind potential challenges with tax issues, legal issues and general administration work. If these challenges are tackled productively, then the rewards (or ROI) gained should be great. The following management consultancies may be able to assist – it is worth doing the research. Only the main China head office of each company is provided; they will be able to advise on where you can go from there.

Accenture China (Beijing)
7/F, Capital Tower
6A, Jian Guo Men Wai Avenue
Chaoyang District
Beijing 100022
Tel: +86 (0)10 5870 5870
Fax: +86 (0)10 6561 2077
Website: www.accenture.com

APCO China
16th Floor, NCI Tower
12A Jianguomenwai Avenue
Chaoyang District
Beijing 100022
People's Republic of China
Phone: +86 (0)10 6505 5128
Fax: +86 (0)10 6505 5258
Website: beijing@apcoworldwide.com

2

A.T. Kearney (Shanghai) Management Consulting Co., Ltd.
HSBC Bldg., 42nd Floor
1000 Lujiazui Ring Road
Pudong New Area
Shanghai 200120
P.R. China
Tel: +86 (0)21 6841 2020
Website: www.atkearney.com

Bain & Company Consulting Group- China
Unit 2407-09, Office Tower 2
China Central Place
79 Jianguo Road
Chaoyang District
Beijing 100025 China
Tel: +86 (0)10 6533 1199
Fax: +86 (0)10 6598 9090
Website: www.bain.com

BearingPoint
Shanghai (China Headquarter)
31F CITIC Square
1168 West Nanjing Road
Shanghai 200041
P.R. China
Tel: +86 (0)21 5292 5392
Fax: +86 (0)21 5292 5391

Booz Allen Hamilton China
Suite 2511, One Corporate Ave
222 Hu Bin Road
Shanghai 200021 China
Tel: +86 (0)21 6340 6633
Fax: +86 (0)21 6340 6048
Website: www.boozallen.cn

Boston Consulting Group China
21/F, Central Plaza
227 Huangpi Bei Lu
Shanghai, 200003 CHINA
Phone: +86 (0)21 2306 4000
Fax: +86 (0)21 6375 8628
Website: www.bcggreaterchina.com

2

CapGemini China
Unit 803-806
Capital Tower
5 Jia JianGuoMenwai Avenue
Chao Yang District, Beijing
Tel: +86 (0)10 6563 7388
Fax: +86 (0)10 6563 7399
Website: www.cn.capgemini.com

Deloitte China
Deloitte Touche Tohmatsu CPA Ltd.
8/F Office Tower W2
The Towers, Oriental Plaza
1 East Chang An Avenue
100738 Beijing, China
Tel: + 86 (0)10 8520 7788
Fax: + 86 (0)10 8518 1218
Website: www.deloitte.com

Droege Management Consultants China
Rm. 2001 Green Land Commercial Centre
1258 Yu Yuan Road
Shanghai 200050
PR China
Tel.:   +86 (0)21 6240 9090
Fax: +86 (0)21 6240 9881
Website: www.droege.de

EAC Management Consulting
Novel Plaza, Rm. 1403
128 Nanjing West Road
200003 Shanghai
P.R. of China
Phone: +86-21-63508150
Fax: +86-21-63508151
E-mail: eac-sha@eac-consulting.de
Website: www.eac-consulting.de

Fiducia Management Consultants
Unit 0603, Landmark Tower 2
8 North Dongsanhuan Road,
Chaoyang District
Beijing, 100004, China
Tel: +86 (0)10 6590 6108/6220
Fax: +86 (0)10 6590 6109

E-mail: info@fiducia-china.com
Website: www.fiducia-china.com

Far Eastern Limited China
Rm315-319, 3 Floor,
HuaLian Development Mansion,
728, XinHua Rd.,
200052 Shanghai, China
Tel: +86 (0)21 6283 3322
Fax: +86 (0)21 6283 2277
E-Mail: Shanghai@far-eastern.cn
Website: www.far-eastern.de

JLJ Management Consultants China
Unit 603-605
Shanghai Oriental Center
699 Nanjing West Road / 31 Wujiang Road
Shanghai China 200041
Tel   +86 (0)21 5211 0068
Fax   +86 (0)21 5211 0069
Email: info@jljgroup.com
Website: www.jljgroup.com

LEK Management Consultants
Floor 34, CITIC Square
1168 Nanjing Road West
Shanghai, 200041
China
Tel: +86 (0)21 6122 3900
Fax: +86 (0)21 6122 3988
E-mail: info@lek.com
Website: www.lek.com

McKinsey China
17/F Platinum Building
233 Tai Cang Road
Shanghai 200020
Peoples Republic of China
Tel: +86 (0)21 6385 8888
Fax: +86 (0)21 6386 2000
Website: www.mckinsey.com

Mercer Investment Consulting/HR Consulting China
Room 3601
Hong Kong New World Tower
300 Huaihai Zhong Road

People's Republic of China
200021
Tel: +86 (0)21 6335 3358
Fax: +86 (0)21 6361 6533
Website: www.merceric.com
Website: www.mercerhr.com

Monitor Consulting China
Unit 3905-3906, K. Wah Center
1010 Middle Huaihai Road
Xuhui District
Shanghai 200031
China
Tel   +86 (0)21 6145 8900
Fax   +86 (0)21 6145 8901
Website: www.monitorgroup.com.cn

PWC China
11/F PricewaterhouseCoopers Center
202 Hu Bin Road
Shanghai 200021, PRC
Tel: +86 (0)21 6123 8888
Fax: +86 (0)21 6123 8800
Website: www.pwc.com

Roland Berger Strategy Consultants (Shanghai) Ltd
23rd Floor Shanghai Kerry Center
1515 Nanjing West Road
Shanghai 200040
China
Tel: +86 (0)21 5298 6677
Fax: +86 (0)21 5298 6660
E-mail: office_shanghai@rolandberger.com
Website: www.rolandberger.com.cn

Focusing on your market

Government and
management
agencies

Upon the conclusion of your initial research on the China
market, there may be a need for you to investigate further
any specialist areas which you feel would not otherwise
be covered by government or management agencies, such
as a detailed economic review of specific industrial
sectors. There are myriad options available such as
Bloomberg (www.bloomberg.com), the *Economist*
(www.economist.com) and Reuters (www.reuters.com).

Many of these companies provide quite a lot of useful up to date information these days on China. The world's attention these days is so firmly focused on the emerging economies of China and India, that it is hard to find a single day when China is not mentioned in their publications or on the homepages of their websites.

Two of the most popular and widely acclaimed agencies in the industry for economic analysis are Dun & Bradstreet (D&B) and The Economic Intelligence Unit (EIU). D&B offer a detailed, web based information service to businesses and individuals on their industry. D&B offer many in-house publications, from which there are a number of excellent reads that businesses thinking of moving into China might find useful.

The first one is the *International Risk & Payment Review*, which provides a detailed analysis of political, commercial and economic risks, and covers over 130 countries, including China. It is available on an annual subscription with monthly editions. The second is the *Exporter's Encyclopedia*, an annual publication that provides detailed analysis and advice on exporting to countries around the world. There is also the *Market Profile Analysis and Community Profile Analysis*, which provides a geographically based market analysis of specific industries by country.

Political, commercial and economic risks

D&B Corporation HQ
103 JFK Parkway
Short Hills, NJ 07078
Tel: +1 973 921 5500
Website: www.dnb.com

D&B UK
35 Wilson Street
London EC2A 1PX
Tel: (Marlow Office): +44 (0)1628 492000
Website: www.dnb.co.uk

D&B China
Room 501, 5/F, Tower C2
The Towers, Oriental Plaza,
No.1, East Chang An Ave.
Dong Cheng District,

2

Beijing, 100738
Tel: +86 (0)10 8518 5636
Fax: +86 (0)10 8518 7030
E-mail: dnbCHN@dnb.com
Website: www.dnbasia.com/cn

The Economic Intelligence Unit (EIU) is part of the *Economist* group and provides annually and quarterly published journals which give a political and economic overview of the China market. They also provide a special section on emerging markets (India, China and Brazil being the big three on the list), where members can browse through the latest developments in sectors such as tourism, residential property reviews, IP status and so on.

Asia & Australasia
Economist Intelligence Unit
60/F Central Plaza
18 Harbour Road
Hong Kong
Tel: +852 2585 3888
E-mail: hongkong@eiu.com
Website: www.eiu.com

Europe, Middle East & Africa
Economist Intelligence Unit
26 Red Lion Square
London WC1R 4HQ
United Kingdom
Tel: +44(0)20 7576 8134
E-mail: london@eiu.com
Website: www.eiu.com

The Americas
Economist Intelligence Unit
111 West 57th Street
New York NY 10019
USA
Tel: +1 212 554 0600
E-mail: newyork@eiu.com
Website: www.eiu.com

The Economic
Intelligence Unit

Global think-tanks

The following organizations are think tanks that discuss current world affairs and other useful issues. They both have a dedicated panel of experts within their organization that focuses on China, as well as other emerging markets. It may be worthwhile to browse these websites and gather any research or get questions answered on China. **Chatham House**, based in London, has been the home of the Royal Institute of International Affairs for over eight decades. Their mission is to be a world-leading source of independent analysis, informed debate and influential ideas on how to build a prosperous and secure world for all. The Chatham House website contains news and updates on free trade, agriculture and global markets. The **Council of Foreign Relations** (CFR), based in New York and Washington, is an online resource for businesses and individuals who want to keep up to date with any foreign policy issues, as well as import & export.

Globalisation Institute
www.globalisation.eu

Council on Foreign Relations
www.cfr.org

Business Monitor International (BMI)

BMI was established in the UK in 1984 and specialises in providing detailed market intelligence reports for corporations worldwide. They also produce essential reports on political risk analysis, financial markets analysis, and macroeconomic forecasts on 175 global markets.

Business Monitor International
Mermaid House
2 Puddle Dock
Blackfriars
London EC4V 3DS, UK
Tel: +44 (0)20 7248 0468
Fax: +44 (0)20 7248 0467
Website: www.businessmonitor.com

2

Chatham House

CFR

BMI

2

Magazines

There are a number of trade magazines that might be worth reading beforehand. Some of these are published by various Chambers of Commerce or by Diplomatic missions.

Croner, part of the Wolters Kluwer (UK) group, produces literature on international trade. Croner also has a dedicated section on their website that provides detailed information on international import and export procedures.

Croner
145 London Road
Kingston Upon Thames
Surrey
KT2 6SR
Tel: +44 (0)208 547 3333
Fax: +44 (0)208 547 2638

Website: www.tradeinternational-centre.net
(this leads to the relevant trade section on the main website of www.croner.co.uk)

Other useful publications are:
China Britain Trade Review
Published by the CBBC (www.cbbc.org)

Hong Kong Trader Highlights
Published by the Hong Kong TDC (www.tdctrade.com)

Overseas Trade
Published by the UK Trade and Investment
(www.uktradeinvest.gov.uk)

China Economic Review
Published by Alain Charles Publishing Ltd
(www.chinaeconomicreview.com)

International Trade Today
Published by the Institute if Export (www.export.org.uk)

A list of useful websites is provided in Appendix 1.

Travel advice and media

Detailed information on transport to China, visas, flights etc. is provided in Chapter 3. For sound, up-to-the-minute travel advice it is best to get in contact with your Embassy or Consulate-General where you are are staying, or visit your Embassy's website. A list of some foreign diplomatic missions in China is provided in this chapter and also in Appendix A.

Information on media channels available in China is listed under the communications section in Chapter four. If however you are interested in business opportunities involving advertising or filming in China, then the best approach is to speak to the Chinese Embassy or Chinese Consulate-General in your country before you leave for China. They would be able to advise you on the necessary paperwork required to film in China.

Receiving permission from the Chinese government to film is often difficult, and can sometimes take months. It is best to win trust from the authorities by talking to them about the nature of your film and what locations you hope to use. It is best not to go around making series or programmes in secret but rather to be honest and open with the government and the people you will be filming. Always ask people if they are happy to be filmed or photographed.

The BBC World Service broadcasts throughout the world in English and 32 other languages. A significant part of their remit covers developments in British industry, science and technology.

BBC World Service broadcasts

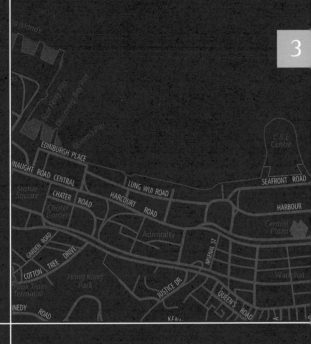

3

getting to China

getting to China

The various considerations
in arranging travel to China

On the whole, global air travel is on the increase; nowhere is this more apparent than in China. With the opening of new International airports in cities such as Guangzhou, Shenzhen and Dalian, it has become much easier for people to travel to China from Europe, America or other far away destinations with fewer connections than previously. It goes without saying that the business traveller has slightly different requirements than those that would apply to a tourist. These will include being able to get from A to B within a set amount of time, comfortably and without the hassle of rushing through busy airports with all of your luggage. For these reasons you may prefer to travel Business class rather than the usual 'Cattle Class' as Economy class is referred to sometimes. There are a number of travel agents that cater for the business minded individual, and they usually tend to offer special 'Business class travel' discounts to corporations.

Business class

Flying to China or Hong Kong usually takes about 12 hours Non-Stop from Europe (13-15 Hours with connecting flights), while from North America it can take anything from 15 Hours to 17 hours Non-Stop, or a couple of hours more with connecting flights – these times vary depending on if flying from the East Coast or the West Coast of North America.

When travelling to China or Hong Kong from Europe, most flights leave in the evening or at night and arrive the following day when it is afternoon in Asia. It is best to schedule yourself on these flights because you can at least get some well-deserved sleep overnight. The only downside is that you will have to force yourself to go to sleep again when you arrive in Hong Kong or China as it will already be around seven or eight in the evening when you have checked into your hotel or reached your expatriate home. Travelling on a Friday or at the weekend will give you enough time to recover from any jetlag.

It's always good to plan your journey well ahead of time when flying within China as well. In fact you can get around most of SE Asia within 3 hours flying time. Flying times between Hong Kong and Beijing are roughly 3 hours, although from experience I can tell you that this

3

can easily turn into 5 hours if there is a slight hint of fog or rain! Most people leave one day off for travelling between cities and so planning is crucial in being able to maximize your time for meetings or being entertained by your hosts.

Major international airports in China

You need to pay airport tax when you depart from any city in China. In 2008, departure tax on all domestic flights was fifty Yuan (Approx. US$7.00) and for International flights it was ninety Yuan (Approx. US$13.00). You need to pay the airport tax at the booth near check-in unless it is already included in your ticket. In Hong Kong and Macau, you don't need to pay the departure tax and it's normally included in your ticket price. In 2008, the Departure tax from both Macau and Hong Kong airports was equivalent to HK$50. Most European and North American Airlines fly to the following major cities in China:

Departure Tax

Beijing
The capital's only passenger airport, Beijing Capital International Airport, is located approximately 28km to the northeast of the city centre. On average every year, over sixty international and domestic airlines use the airport. In 2008 Beijing airport handled more than twenty-nine million passengers. The national flag carrier, Air China, has its HQ based at Beijing Airport.

All well known International Airlines fly to Beijing including: British Airways, American Airlines, Continental, KLM, Air France, Lufthansa, SAS, Austrian Airlines, Air India, Singapore Airlines, Qantas and Emirates. www.bcia.com.cn Official website of Beijing Airport

Guangzhou
Guangzhou Baiyun International airport is situated 32km to the northwest of the city centre, with connections to major cities in five continents as well as many domestic flights. China Southern Airlines has its head office at Baiyun airport. International airlines flying to Guangzhou include: Air France, Lufthansa,

Northwest Airlines and Kenya Airways.
www.baiyunairport.com – Official Website of Guangzhou
Baiyun Airport

Hong Kong

Hong Kong International Airport, 'Chep Lap Kok', is
located on the outskirts of the city on Lantau Island.
Prior to 1997, Hong Kong's airport was located in the
middle of the city with the runway stretching out into
Kowloon Bay. It used to be famous for having the
most dangerous landing procedures for pilots because
planes used to make daring 33 degrees approaches and
passengers could easily see people's washing hanging
on the balconies as the plane came in to land!

All major international airlines fly to Hong Kong and
it is one of the best and most modern airports in the
world. Hong Kong is the base for Cathay Pacific
Airways, and Dragon Airlines.
www.hongkongairport.com – Official website of Hong
Kong Airport

Macau

Macau's International Airport is also built on an Island,
just like Hong Kong Airport. The airport is not busy and
is mainly used for Charter or Cargo flights. Air Macau,
the national carrier, is based here.
www.macau-airport.gov.mo – Macau International
Airport website

Shanghai

Shanghai has two major international airports,
Hongqiao and Pudong. You would most likely be using
Pudong airport as Hongqiao is used for domestic flights.
Pudong is also the base and HQ of China Eastern
Airlines. Over forty world-wide airlines use the airport
with an annual average passenger capacity of nineteen
million (2007 Figures).
www.shanghaiairport.com – Both Pudong and Hongqiao
airports use this website

Shenzhen

Shenzhen has one major international airport, Bao-an
International airport, which is located 32km to the
northwest of the city centre, near the Pearl Delta, with

3

connections to major Asian cities as well as many domestic flights. Shenzhen has its own airline, Shenzhen Airlines, with numerous daily flights to destinations within China and several Asian cities.

Although Shenzhen airport is an international airport, the majority of the flights outside China are to destinations elsewhere in the Asia Pacific region. There is a regular daily helicopter service to Macau operated from the airport.
www.szairport.com – The official website of Shenzhen airport

Visas

All foreigners entering China need to have a valid visa in hand. A Chinese Tourist Visa is more readily available than a Business Visa. Foreigners relocating to China for work purposes, first need to obtain a tourist visa valid for 30 days – once they are in China, their employer will arrange all the paperwork involved in getting a Z-type Work Visa. To obtain a Tourist Visa, you should allow at least 3 full working days for processing. Business Visa are usually issued upon an invitation by your host company in China. You will also need a completed application form, a company letter signed by your senior management, a passport sized photograph and a valid return air ticket. The Chinese Embassy may also ask you to produce proof of sufficient funds for your trip to China. All of these materials should be presented with you passport, which should be valid for at least six months after the date of your planned departure from China.

Business Visa

Citizens of most countries can enter Hong Kong and Macau without a visa for up to six months; please check this with your high commission or with the Chinese Embassy in your country. British citizens can enter Hong Kong without a visa for up to six months, whereas American citizens are restricted to three months without a visa. Other countries' time limits vary, and some countries' citizens will require visas – so please check. All foreigners wishing to work in Hong Kong or Macau require a work permit. For more information, you can make enquiries with your corporation about this, or visit the following website (Hong Kong Immigration Department): www.immd.gov.hk

Trade missions

An option available to the first time corporate visitor to China or Hong Kong (especially the former), is to participate in one of the many regular trade missions to these markets. These are excellent networking opportunities and provide 'peace of mind' for the visitor because these missions take the hassle out by arranging hotels, booking flights, arranging visas and so on. There is a set itinerary which may also include some sightseeing.

An important element of a Trade Mission is the Briefing Meeting, usually given by a senior member of the commercial section at the Embassy or Consulate. This talk is useful because it provides an insight into the country, covering issues such as politics, economics, local culture, and the general dos and don'ts for business and non-business related activities in China. There are opportunities to ask questions about trade, or make any non-business related queries. There may be a reception included at the diplomatic mission's office in the evening, and this will provide an excelent opportunity for networking with like-minded individuals.

Information about any forthcoming Trade Missions to China may be obtained from your Embassy, High-Commission, Trade & Industry Office or any local government organisation. Normally corporate websites, magazines and other forms of internal communications are used to advertise such Trade Missions. Every year many foreign governments and political parties arrange Trade Missions to China.

Exhibitions, forums and conferences

We take for granted that almost everything we see today in the West is 'Made in China'. Those goods that are

Briefing meeting

3

designed and manufactured in China are then advertised, promoted and eventually sold in bulk quantity in exhibitions, forums and conferences all over China.

All the major cities in China have at least two to three large exhibition halls because of the great demand for them – with this in mind it is no surprise that China hosts more trade exhibitions than any other country in the world.

Hong Kong has the famous Hong Kong Convention & Exhibition Centre (HKCEC, www.hkcec.com.hk), which is located on the harbour front in Wanchai and has hosted many high profile events, including the World Trade Organisation Conference in 2006.

For future information on any forthcoming Exhibitions in China concerning your industry or area of interest, visit your Chamber of Commerce's website or the Trade & Industry website of your country.

When to go to China

Holidays in China are not the same as in other parts of the world, especially in Europe or North America, so planning your trip to China beforehand, so as not to clash with any Chinese holidays, is advisable.
A full list of public holidays in China is provided in Chapter four. It would be advisable to avoid planning your business trip around Chinese New Year (seven days around the end of January) and the Mid Autumn Festival (seven days in the first week of October). It becomes more complicated with Hong Kong, because in Hong Kong they also celebrate Christmas and New Year just like in other Christian countries, so they have Chinese and Western holidays.

Chinese New Year

Health care

All foreigners wanting to work in China are required to take a full body medical check-up before a work visa is issued; including tests for HIV, Hepatitis B, Syphilis and ECG/Ultrasound. You will be issued with a Certificate of Health Examination in paper form and as a booklet. The

3

paper certificate needs to be handed to the PSB when applying for the work permit, while the booklet form should be kept with your passport at all times in case of inspection.

China has one of the world's highest incidences of Hepatitis B and HIV. With the former on the rise, especially in migrant cities such as Shenzhen; where it was reported by the *Shenzhen Daily newspaper* on World AIDS day in 2007 that there has been a 35% rise of HIV infections within one year. Recently there have also been worries about Bird Flu and SARS.

Chinese medicine

Chinese medicine is widely acknowledged in many western countries and is recognised by the World Health Organisation (WHO, www.who.org). It is based around the idea that a healthy body is one in which the 'internal energies' that flow along the body (known as Qi) try to balance the temperature of your system between hot and cold.

The normal procedure is for your Chinese doctor to observe the colour your tongue and the rate of your pulse and then determine whether your body belongs to the 'hot' or 'cold' set of energies. This is similar to the ancient Chinese philosophy of 'Yin' (Passive energy) and 'Yang' (Active energy) where Yin applies to such things as cold and female and Yang applies to hot and male.

'Yin' and 'Yang'

Always ask your doctor if the herbal medicine has any side effects as Chinese bodies handle herbal medicine differently to western bodies. Normally Chinese doctors will shrug off any problems and give it you anyway. You may want to try Chinese medicine during your stay – and while you should exercise caution, you can have peace of mind that using Chinese medicine will not make your illness worse. The more likely effect is that it will take longer to cure your symptoms or have no discernable effect whatsoever.

3

Hotels

According to data from the China National Tourism Administration, at the end of 2007, China had a total of 16,000 tourist hotels. 970 of these tourist hotels were foreign-funded. Hotel costs in China vary depending on the quality; in China, hotels (even five star hotels) are generally much cheaper than in the West, and if booked within China, even internationally renowned five star hotels can be reserved at an even cheaper price. Hotel standards in Hong Kong and Macau are comparable to any international hotel in the world, and some can be quite pricy. On the mainland however, it is a different story. Staying in a high quality five or four star hotel does make a good impression with your host and makes your stay a comfortable one too – especially if you have been flying for the past 16 hours and need a well deserved rest before an important meeting. It also makes it easier for business visitors to come and visit you for a first time meeting.

Naturally when there are trade days then the costs may increase up to anything from (at least as a ball park figure) 700RMB for 5-star quality hotels and from around 200RMB for a simple 2 or 3 star hotel.

Hotel prices of all quality standards can be high during trade shows, exhibitions and conferences. However you should have no problems if booking your hotel through your trade delegation as most of the costs would be incurred by your company, and companies do get special discounts for group bookings in advance. In China you may also need to be aware of Hotels that may display, say 4-stars, but in actual fact would probably not even be classified as a 3-star standard. But, again, you will only find this with non-international standard hotels and those that have no affiliation with foreign companies.

Quality standards

Almost all Hotels in China are clean and modern by international standards. It should also be borne in mind that the Chinese want to take the first opportunity to make a lasting good impression on a first time visitor – so they take special care in ensuring that your stay is as comfortable as possible. Most hotels in China provide extras free of charge, such as razors and shaving cream, toothpaste and toothbrush (the former can sometimes taste like cough medicine in some hotels but gets the job done anyway), disposable slippers, bathrobes and even a mosquito net in the summer (this can be pulled to surround your bed).

What to take

This all depends on what time of year you are travelling and more importantly which part of China you are going to. If you are going to south China during the winter then there is no need to pack too many warm clothes because actual winter in southern China lasts no more than two months at the worst and majority of the year is warm and humid. On the other hand, winter time can present some exceedingly freezing conditions in the northern cities such as Beijing, Shanghai and Xian for example.

Take sensible amounts of clothes with you depending on how long you will be staying in China. At the end it all comes down to personal choice and of course when on business its always best to structure your belongings so you don't need to panic at the last minute in case there are more meetings or you need to change your suit for a formal dinner party with Tuxedo and so on.

If you are an expat who is relocating to China for a longer period, then you may be able to claim 'relocation allowance' (anything from six months and beyond is considered as 'long period'). While other corporations offer the option for you to carry extra luggage on top of the basic amount that airlines offer (typically this extra luggage can be anything from 80kg up to 180kg, depending on your company's policy). It would be advisable to move as many personal belongings as you like and make the most of the allowance that is given to you.

Relocation allowance

Take some medication with you, especially if you know that it may be difficult to purchase in China. Although most medications are readily available in China, there may be exceptions (for Epilepsy and Asthma for example) and it may not be available in China so check with your GP and doctor in your home country before taking a reasonable quantity to China. It may be the case that you are limited to a certain number of prescribed

3

Medication

tablets that you can get over the counter
at one time. If so, you will need to arrange the delivery
of further prescriptions.

Finally, it would be wise to get valid insurance (health
or otherwise) before you go to China. Normally as an
expatriate, your company should be able to arrange
this for you. Most expats usually have BUPA Gold
Health Insurance as well as other insurance schemes
arranged by their organisation. Otherwise carry out the
research in your country before you leave for China, as

Health insurance

it can be difficult to get insurance once you are in the
country (details for insurance in China are listed in
Chapter Four).

4

the ground rules

the ground rules

This section takes the reader by the hand and talks through the nitty-gritty of everyday life, from how to get around to how much to tip the bell-boy. Knowledge of these essentials provides the confidence to go out and do business effectively.

Currency

The official currency of mainland China is the Yuan. Although the official code is CNY, the currency is also commonly abbreviated 'RMB' for Renminbi – or 'People's Money'. Yuan in Chinese literally means a 'round object' or 'round coin' as the original Chinese money considered of iron rings that had a square or round hole in the middle. When pronounced correctly, the word 'Yuan' sounds like U-AN. One Yuan is divided into 10 Jiao or Mao. One Mao is divided into 10 Fen. In Cantonese, Jiao and fen are called Ho and Sin. Although with almost everyone speaking good English in Hong Kong, you will seldom need to use these terms.

China's currency was once set at a rate of 8.28 RMB to one US dollar, making one Yuan worth about twelve cents, and one Jiao (or ten fen) worth about one cent. However, in July 2005, China finally ended its decade old peg to the dollar allowing the Yuan to fluctuate against a basket of foreign currencies. This was a welcome sight for many western economies, as well as for the European Commission, which closely monitored the talks with the Chinese government. Now the Yuan is seen next to other currencies at Bureau–de-change counters around the world. In 2008, the average value of US$1 was equal to approximately 7.58 RMB, with the year ending on a low of 7.38 RMB for 1 US$.

The Bank of China, ICBC and the China Merchants Bank all have foreign exchange counters. You should not have any difficulty exchanging currency or American Express Travellers' cheques in the majority of the western banks or at any approved hotel. In 2008, the maximum amount of hard currency you could take out of China was 20,000 RMB (equivalent to approx $2500).

Banks

The five main Banks in China are as follows:

Agricultural Bank of China
Global HQ
Jia 23, Fuxing Road
Beijing, China, 100036
Tel: +86 (0)10 6821 6807/ 6842 4439

4

Money

4

Fax: +86 (0)10 6829 7160/ 6842 4437
Website: www.abchina.com

Bank of China (The main state owned bank)
Bank of China Global HQ
1 Fuxingmen Nei Dajie,
Beijing 100818, China
Swift: BKCH CN BJ
Tlx: +86 (0)10 22254
Tel: +86 (0)10 66596688
Fax: +86 (0)10 66593777
Website: www.bank-of-china.com

China Merchants Bank
Global HQ
News Palaza
2 Mid Shen Nan Road
Fu Tian District
Shenzhen, China
Website: www.cmbchina.com

Construction Bank of China
24 Hour hotline: 95533
Website: www.ccb.cn

ICBC (State Owned)
Global HQ
55 FuXingMenNei Street
Xicheng District
Beijing, 100032, P.R.C
Nationwide 24-hour Service Hotline: 95588
E-mail: webmaster@icbc.com.cn
Website: www.icbc.com.cn

ICBC

ICBC is the largest lender in mainland China. In the early
part of 2007 it also began applying for International
banking licences for USA and Russia (with plans to
open branches in the latter in the early part of 2008). It
managed to secure a deal, in October of 2007, for 20 per
cent of Standard Bank in South Africa for an estimated
US$6 million. While foreign banks have been making
significant inroads into the booming Chinese economy in
recent years and pushing hard for access; Chinese banks
have been excluded from foreign markets. This is simply
due to a history of poor risk management and corporate

governance. Foreign interest in ICBC has been strong too, with American Express investing over US$200 million in 2006. With a market capitalisation of US$254 billion, ICBC officially became the world's most valuable bank after a strong gain in its share price, overtaking Citigroup.

4

Bank of China

The Bank of China is the only one of the nation's state owned lenders that has any significant offshore presence – with the vast majority of its operations being in Hong Kong and Macau. If you are coming to China through your employer in your country, then your employer should be able to assist you in setting up a bank account for your salary and personal income. Credit cards are widely accepted in Hong Kong and Macau, and, although not often used, they are beginning to be accepted at major shops and outlets on the mainland.

As a new account holder in China, you can only open a credit card account if you are Chinese and have a property in China. Further details may be obtained from the www.bankofchina.com

Most of the banks in mainland China are open seven days a week and are busy with long queues. Cash machines are available everywhere just like in the West.

International banking

Since the year 2000, there has been an increase in the number of western banks in the major cities in China. HSBC, Citibank and Standard Chartered Bank have branches in all the major cities (Guangzhou, Shenzhen, Beijing and Shanghai). There are plans for theses banks to open branches in other cities in the next few years. There are also plans for new western banks to open branches in the major cities.

American Express has branches in Beijing, Guangzhou and Shanghai. In 2007, American Express also put forward a proposal to open branches in other cities across China, including Shenzhen.

4

Money transfer

International Money transfer is possible with Western Union. Most Post Offices have a Western Union counter inside their branches. The procedure is simple and does not take long. www.westernunion.com

Transport in China

Gone are the days when China was known as the land of bicycles. These days it's all about planes, trains and automobiles – and there are plenty of all three here. Taxis, and the general traffic on the road are susceptible to jams as soon as there is any sign of rain – so expect delays if it is raining. Queues at airports (for passengers and planes waiting to depart) and train stations can be very long indeed.

Air travel

Flying domestically in China has steadily become cheaper than before, and there is plenty of choice of flight times and destinations. During off-peak seasons flights can usually be bought at the last minute for a reasonable price.

Until 1979, air travel in China was a rarity and only reserved for wealthy businessmen or those in the government. There was only one airline (CAAC or Air China as it is known today) and both the airspace and airports were under the control of the military. All of that changed when Den Xiaoping opened the way to make air travel in China commonplace for everyone. Nowadays all control of airlines is administered by the Civil Aviation Administration of China (CAAC).

Despite China already having too many airlines (28 in 2008) and too many airports (467 in 2008), the government has plans for further airports to be opened in rural and remote areas, as well as more private airlines. This will make it easier for everyone to fly around in China at affordable rates. Tickets are available either at travel agents throughout the country, at airline offices (listed in this book) or at the airport. One problem that you may encounter is that in most places airline tickets can only be paid for in cash, although some travel agents are starting to accept credit cards. The main problem experienced by foreigners is flights being delayed or cancelled without explanation.

Unlike at Hong Kong airport, where the ground staff are exceedingly efficient in getting planes to meet their departure slots, airports in mainland China have quiet a way to go before those standards are matched. The quality of service has also improved in recent times, with airline catering companies recruiting expats who specialise in nothing but airline food to try to improve the standards.

Private jets – For the corporate executive

The beauty of private jet travel is that travellers can go anywhere, any time of day without the hassle of aircraft delays. Many economic pundits reckon that China is set to be a booming market for private jets in the next 10 to 15 years, especially after the Beijing Olympics and other important events happening in this remarkable era of China's rising economy.

Already there are numerous private companies such as Deer jet (www.deerjet.com) and Metrojet Executive Travel (www.metrojet.com), that offer the privilege to senior company executives of getting from one part of China to the other in a cost efficient, hassle free and timely way. If a senior executive wants to get from Shenzhen to Xian (which takes about 3 hours flying time non-stop) to attend an important meeting that could make or break a deal, and his meeting is in the afternoon, then taking an executive jet would be the best option because there would be no delays, no queues at check in desks, no need to waste time at immigration, security or baggage reclaim (all of which can easily add on another 4 hours in addition to the 3 hours flying time). Some executives already take advantage of private jets but this is set to increase dramatically in the future as China breeds new high-flying senior executives who value their time.

Bicycles

In China, sadly and ironically, the bicycle – once the only mode of transport available for the millions of inhabitants – is a vanishing breed. Nevertheless, the

4

bicycle is still very much used, and when you see someone riding a bike in Beijing you think to yourself 'Ah, now I'm in China!' It is nice to have that feeling of seeing something that was so closely connected with the country for many years. Foreigners can ride bicycles in China, but need to register their bikes with the local Public Security Bureau (PSB). Basic rules apply such as, avoid dirty and rocky tracks that could easily puncture your tires (although this is hard to avoid in rural areas) and also get yourself a secure lock. As a foreigner you may be a likely target for thieves if your bike is new and expensive!

Buses and coaches

If you are on business trip then there may be no need or time for you to try the local buses and coaches, but they are for the most part both clean and comfortable, and a cheap way to travel and see the country.

Some buses and coaches also have televisions that play Chinese movies or songs. Bottled water is provided free of charge on coaches which operate on longer routes.

Metro and trains

China has one of the world's most modern fleets of metro trains (mostly manufactured by Siemens or Bombardier Canada). All Metro trains in China are clean, spacious, with convenient signs in both English and Chinese and are air conditioned – which is a relief, especially in the summer. On board announcements in both trains and metros, are made in Chinese and English.

Trains in China are still the preferred way of travel over long distance for the vast majority of the population, and more so during the national holidays when seats need to be booked well in advance. As opposed to air travel, trains in China are exceedingly efficient in getting off the station platform on time. Trains for long distance journeys are not as overcrowded as they used to be (exceptions can still be made for the hard seat compartments!) as only passengers with seat bookings are accommodated onboard.

Taxis in China

Taxis are metered and available twenty-four hours a day throughout the country. There is no need to book in advance or go to a designated taxi stand as all can be hailed on the street. Available taxies have a bright red light displayed on their front panel behind the windscreen.

Most taxi drivers cannot converse in English, so it is best to get a colleague or your hotel concierge to write down your destination in Chinese so you can show it to the taxi driver. Most Hotel staff would be pleased to assist you on this matter and you can always show the business card of the hotel or the destination address you want to go to.

Always have small amounts of change for travel by taxi, usually 300 or 400 RMB should be enough in case of emergency. Taxi drivers can refuse to take you if you are drunk and behave rudely. On the whole taxi drivers in China will not cheat you deliberately. Most taxies will have automated receipts printed upon the completion of your journey.

Disabled travellers

For the disabled traveller, most good hotels, schools, offices and housing areas have a ramp for wheelchair users next to the stairs that leads to the lifts. Some Restaurants also have specially made tables for disabled customers. Unlike in some western countries where the buses or taxies have a special drop out ramp at the bottom of the door to allow wheelchair users to get in/out, in China, this kind of facility is not presently available.

There are some facilities for the deaf and blind; I have seen, for example, people using Braille menus in some restaurants in Shanghai. Unfortunately for the disabled traveller, China is a country of steps, walkways, crowded streets and 'Asian style' toilets, which would not be usable by many disabled travellers.

4

4

Shipping

China has just over 2,000 ports, of which 135 are open to foreign ships. Shanghai, Dalian, Shenzhen, Guangzhou and Nanjing are just some of the largest shipping ports. It is estimated the by the year 2010, over a third of the world's shipping will originate from ports in China.

There are three main sectors of shipping in China:

International Seafreight: On mainland China the leader is COSCO (www.cosco.com.cn), which reached over 42 million DWT in 2007, while the dominant company in Hong Kong is OOCL (www.oocl.com).

Coastal Seafreight: The leading company in China is China Shipping Company (www.cnshipping.com). In 2007, it carried approximately 11 million DWT.

River Shipping: The leader here is China Changjiang National Shipping Corporation. (www.china-csc.com) In 2007 it carried about 6 million DWT.

In Guangdong province, Shenzhen's Yantian Port was officially classed as the second largest deep-water container terminal in China in 2008. Many economic think tanks strongly predict that Shenzhen, which is already taking market share from cities such as Hong Kong, Guangzhou and Shanghai in handling China's exports, is well on course to replace these ports as the mainland's largest port.

Communications
E-mail and internet access

China has caught up with the Internet boom quicker than other countries in the East. There is no clatter or confusion when setting up an internet connection at home or in the office. Internet on the mainland is very safe, fast (you can easily get ADSL connection in any town and city – even the rural areas!) and, most importantly, cheap. As of 2008 prices from China Telecom, a year's worth of of unlimited access, with a fast ADSL broadband connection, cost just 600RMB (Approx US$80!). Most good hotels will have an

Broadband

excellent broadband connection in the room, but they tend to be more pricey, costing anything in the region of US$0.30 a minute (Approx 4 RMB).

Broadband is widely available through China Telecom or China Unicom, the two main state owned service providers on the mainland. It's best to take a Chinese speaking friend with you to a local China Telecom store.

When you apply for your Internet access account, it's best to take your passport and a copy of your passport with you. Although you're technically required to register with the Public Security Bureau (PSB) before you can open an account, many ISPs will do this for you.

Internet cafés (Wangba)

Internet cafés are located in all the main cities. Some of them are in coffee houses such as Starbucks or Illy; however the vast majority are situated in dark smelly rooms clouded with cigarette smoke. These are unhygienic and should be avoided if possible. Be careful as some of these internet cafés are operated without a proper license and are prone to random checks by plain clothed police. Costs at the time of writing are about four Yuan per hour.

International calls

You can request to have access to international calls from your home phone when you set up with China Telecom. Making international calls from China, from a Hotel or from your residence, is not cheap, because there is only one provider, and therefore no competition for prices. International calls from Hotels can cost anything from 8RMB ($1USD) a minute. International Calling cards provided by either China Satcom (known as 17970) or by China Unicom (known as 17910) are available at street kiosks in values of 50RMB or 100RMB.

Relocation companies/couriers in China

The use of courier services has increased at a rapid pace in the past five years. The domestic postal services in both Hong Kong and China are by and large efficient, fast and cost effective. Postal stamps can be bought in hotels. Business for international courier companies

4

such as DHL, Fedex and UPS has increased dramatically since they entered the China market in the early 1990's. All of these companies have their offices in the major cities of China.

AGS Four Winds
Corporate website: www.agsfourwings.com
(Has offices in major cities on the mainland)
5/F Len Shing Industrial Centre
4, A Kung Ngam Village Road
Shaukeiwan
Hong Kong, CHINA
Tel: +852 2 885 9666
Fax: +852 2 567 7594
E-mail: enquiries-hongkong@agsfourwinds.com

Allied Pickfords
China Corporate website: www.alliedpickfords.com.cn

Asian Tigers KC Dat (China) Ltd
Corporate website: www.asiantigersgroup.com
CHINA HQ (Beijing)
Room 302, Grand Rock Plaza
13 Xinzhongxili,
Dongcheng District
Beijing, 100027, CHINA
Tel: +86 (0)10 6415 1188
Fax: +86 (0)10 6417 9579
E-mail: general.pek@asiantigers-china.com

Baltrans International Moving
Corporate website: www.bim.com.hk

Beijing Friendship Packing and Transportation Company
5 Xiliu Jie Sanlitun, Beijing, CHINA
Tel: +86 (0)10-532-4375/532-4827

Columbia International removals
Corporate website: www.columbia-removals.com.hk
Specializes in international & local household removals, fine art services, office relocation, household items & documents storage, total logistics solutions
Room 2213 Hong Kong Plaza
188 Connaught Road West
Hong Kong Plaza

Tel: +852 2547-6228
Fax: +852 2858-2418
E-mail: info@columbia-removals.com.hk

Crown Relocations
Corporate website: www.crownrelo.com
Have warehouses and offices in 8 satellite cities in China
(and Hong Kong). All of which have connections to any
city or town within Greater China.
Room 201, West Tower
Golden Bridge Bldg.
1a Jianguomenwai Dajie
Beijing,China,100020
Tel: +86 (0)10-65850640
Fax: +86 (0)10-65850648
Email: china@crownrelo.com

DHL CHINA
Corporate website: www.cn.dhl.com
DHL-Sinotrans Ltd. (Joint Venture)
45 Xinyuan St.
Chaoyang District
Beijing, 100027, CHINA
Tel: +86 (0)10 6466 5566

Federal Express International
Website: www.fedex.com

Kuehne & Nagel Global Relocation
Corporate website: www.kuehne-nagel.com
The Kuehne + Nagel network in China comprises 21
strategically located office and warehouse locations,
offering comprehensive supply chain solutions to a fast -
growing local and international customer base. Kuehne +
Nagel in China is part of the worldwide Kuehne + Nagel
Group, which has 830 offices in more than 100 countries.
Kuehne & Nagel Beijing Office
26 Xiaoyun Road
Beijing, Chaoyang District
Beijing, China, 100016
Tel: +86 (0)10 84580908
Fax: +86 (0)10 84585315
info.beijing@kuehne-nagel.com

4

4

Links Relocations
Corporate website: www.linksrelo.com
Links Relocation Hong Kong Office
Rm. A-C, 11/F, Champion Building,
287-291 Des Voeux Road
Central, Hong Kong
Tel: +852 2366 6700
Fax: +852 2366 6400
Email: links@linksrelo.com

Overseas Moving Network International (OMNI)
Santa Fe Relocation Services Co. Ltd.
Corporate website: www.santaferelo.com
Santa Fe Relocation Beijing Office
2, Street No. 8
Beijing Airport Logistics Zone
Beijing 101300, CHINA
Tel: +86 (0)10 6947 0688
Fax: +86 (0)10 6947 0699
E-mail: beijing@santafe.com.cn

Relocasia
Corporate website: www.relocasia.com
Relocasia Hong Kong Office
F2, 13F
Gee Tung Cheong Ind Building
4 Fung Yip Street
Chai Wan
Hong Kong, CHINA
Tel: +852 2976 9969
Fax: +852 2976 9947
E-mail: enquiry@relocasia.com

Sinotrans Global Freight
Corporate website: www.sinotrans.com
Sinotrans Beijing Head Office
Sinotrans Plaza
Xizhimen North St.
Beijing 100044, P.R.China
(Sea Freight)   Tel: +86 (0)10 465 2354
(Rail Freight)   Tel: +86 (0)10 381 4440
(Air Cargo)   Tel: +86 (0)10 501 1014
(Exhibition Transport)   Tel: +86 (0)10 467 1713

UPS CHINA
Corporate website: www.ups.com
UPS Customer Service Center (Call Center)
People's Republic of China
Nationwide Toll Free No: 800-820-8388 /
400-820-8388 (For cell phone user)
Overseas Dial-In: +86 (0)21 3896 5555
Fax: +86 (0)21 5831 0314

4

Media

All international and local media, including the internet, is censored by the central government. External media sites such as the BBC, CNN, Bloomberg etc are accessible but some news pages are blocked by the central server. On certain occasions which involve any sensitive political issues, search engines such as Yahoo and Google may be temporarily blocked. The popular 'Youtube.com' is also blocked in China.

Websites

The state owned television organisation is called CCTV, which stands for 'China Central Television Channel'. CCTV has twelve broadcasting channels, with CCTV 9 (www.cctv-9.com) being the only English language channel available on the mainland and on selected satellite channels throughout the world. There are two English language channels that are available on cable TV, TVB Pearl, which has its HQ at the Pearl Tower in Shanghai, and ATV, which is transmitted from Hong Kong. BBC and CNN are accessible on cable TV in private homes or in four-star and five-star hotels.

Television

China Daily (www.chinadaily.com.cn), is the major English language newspaper and is available in hotels and reception halls of multinationals, but it is difficult to find on the street stall.

The Hong Kong based English daily newspaper is the *South China Morning Post* (www.scmp.com). The SCMP is available in all major hotels, diplomatic missions and multinational offices on the mainland. Most International newspapers and magazines can be bought in Hong Kong and Macau at many newsagents (including International editions of the UK *Sun*, UK *Daily Mirror*, US *Wall Street Journal* and the UK *Financial Times*).

Newspapers

4

Insurance in China

There are many insurance companies in your own country with whom you can get short term insurance if you are going to China for a month or so. If you are being relocated to China by your own company, then usually your corporation will issue you with a good insurance scheme as part of the standard package most expats receive.

Your employer should provided travel, health and all other necessary insurance to you automatically, however if you need insurance for your personal belongs or life assurance for yourself then Ping An Insurance is the best option for you. In China it is no longer compulsory to buy insurance with your mortgage.

The AIA insurance company (www.aia.com.cn), is internationally renowned and have branches in all of the main cities throughout China. China's answer to AIA is the Ping An Insurance group (www.pa18.com), named after the famous Ping An Rice Terraces village in Guangxi Province.

Business etiquette

If you are sent to China as an expatriate on a contract through your employer in your own country then there will be corporate cultural differences which may need to be taken into account. Working for Siemens in Germany will not be the same as working for Siemens in Guangzhou. The corporate way of working, behaving in meetings and dealing with other corporate issues will be localised to the market in which you are working, although the general company ethos, branding and values will remain the same everywhere around the world.

There are a few multinationals that encourage their staff to discuss problems in English and organise team exercises in English. However, language is not the only problem reported by most of the foreign staff members with whom I have worked. Some of the challenges and problems experienced by foreign employees working in China are:

4

- Unlike some companies in the west where you can approach your senior management in an informal way, in China it is quite the opposite. Corporate culture in China is based on a hierarchical structure; therefore you can't just go and see your manager as and when you want to. It is a formal atmosphere and you have to send e-mails or arrange a meeting through the secretary beforehand. Normally this does not apply if you are in a senior management position yourself, again, it depends on the company and the way the senior management of that company works. Some Multinationals have a working policy similar to that of their western offices, while others are such that, even if you are a senior manager, you have to go through the correct procedures before meeting with your boss.

- In many Chinese corporations, the behaviour of the senior management is such that they would do what they deem to be best for their employees. In the past in some Chinese companies it used to be a common thing that if the employees did not agree with the senior management then they would risk being fired on the spot. However this is unlikely in a multinational, and certainly not to foreign employees. Foreign employees on the whole are given a lot of respect by their Chinese counterparts.

- Normal business hours are from 8am until midday and from 2pm until 6pm. Most multinationals will require you to work for only five days, while other companies, including multinationals, will occasionally require their employees to work a six-day week – depending on the structure of the company's HR policy. On the other hand, consider yourself lucky as many of the factory employees along the Shenzhen to Guangzhou industrial belt work the full seven-day week with only the occasional weekend off.

Business hours

- When involved in serious business negotiations about pricing, products, land and so on, it may

4

Interpreters

be helpful to bring along an interpreter who can accompany you to meetings and talks to assist in smooth understanding by both parties (unless you are confident that you can master the Chinese language yourself!). With or without an interpreter, you should speak slowly, clearly and in a polite and friendly manner so that the other party doesn't feel threatened by your requests. Above all else you need to show a great deal of respect as well as trust to your counterparts. After all, you have come to their country to ask them for something, or to offer them something, so there needs to be that element of 'we are in mutual understanding' with each other. Avoid using complicated words, use simple English and above all else pause after every sentence that you speak.

Networking (Guangxi)

In China, networking is known as 'guangxi' and it is an important part of building a good relationship with your Chinese counterparts and other business connections. When attending trade shows or visiting another delegation, it is vitally important that you keep in touch with them in the future as you never know when you may need each other's assistance – whether for business or personal reasons. If you are looking for a business contact to find any professional leads then guangxi can work greatly in your favour. It is very common for friends to consult each other if they know other companies or other expats within corporations who can assist in your business, which can do wonders for the making or breaking of that much needed business idea.

Because all foreigners, and especially business professionals, have something in common in China, when two foreigners converse with each other in the street, or on public transport, then it's a great opportunity to bring together ideas – who knows where your business leads may take you? It could be that golden opportunity to grow your business in China.

One thing that you will have to bear in mind (normally only applies to the men), is that part of the business guangxi ritual may involve participating in the strong drinking culture that exists in China. Generally, the Chinese regard with some degree of doubt anyone who does not participate in the predictable drinking that takes place during almost all business dinners. It doesn't have to be hardcore binge drinking, but even a small glass of wine is enough to give the other party the confidence that you are on the same page as them! It is at these types of social gatherings that most negotiating breakthroughs are made by the major decision makers in multinationals – it is part of the culture. If you want to avoid drinking it is best to make up a medical reason as these are normally accepted without doubt.

Drinking culture

4

Business formalities

The Chinese can be just as formal as the British or the Americans when it comes to corporate business behaviour and dress. In Chinese corporate culture, the norm is to wear conservative suits and ties in subdued colours. Bright colours of any kind are considered rather inappropriate and only for informal occasions such as Chinese New Year or the Mid Autumn festival or in some cases when working at the weekend, when dressing down would be considered acceptable for obvious reasons. Women should wear conservative suits or dresses as well; although it is not a must, generally, a blouse should have a high neckline – especially when working in diplomacy or for multinationals. Stick with subdued, neutral, colours such as beige and brown.

Business attire

Whenever two business people meet for the first time, the formalities are initiated by shaking hands and then exchanging business cards. Although shaking hands is common with everyone, irrespective of age or gender, in business terms it is very important to bear in mind that when you are introduced to a colleague or client, you should stand up to shake hands – this is a way of showing respect to your host, especially if they are senior to you in age or professional hierarchy. Before your visit to meet your Chinese counterpart, it may be a good idea to carry out any essential background reading about Chinese culture, history, and geography. You don't have to go into great detail just some highlight points to show your host that you are aware of the differences will give your host a good impression.

4

It is best to avoid any negativity. If there are points you disagree with, then it is best to politely set these aside by changing the subject or declining in a diplomatic way using 'Maybe' or 'I'll think about it' or 'Yes, that's a good point' and never in a straight 'No'. You will notice that your Chinese host will do the same. When your Chinese colleagues smile or reply with the words 'Not a big problem' or 'The problem is not too serious', then that is a nice way of saying, 'Yes, there are still problems to be managed!' It's a difficult skill which you will have to master – one which is not easy for foreigners to grasp at first because you leave the meeting thinking, 'that was OK' and that both parties made a good impression, whereas the reality is a simple no!

Business cards

Friends, or colleagues who know each other quite well, will often shake hands firmly and for a little bit longer than in Europe or America. When you give someone your business card, it should be held at the top with two hands, and the person who receives the card also takes it with two hands. It is deemed polite to read the card carefully once someone gives it to you, and maybe even try to repeat their name in Chinese and their position. This will give them a feeling of importance in front of their colleagues and will show that you are giving them your absolute attention. If there are a group of people in the meeting then it is polite to go around the table and meet everyone individually. Always bear in mind that losing face for the Chinese is a serious thing, and that giving your host the full attention and respect that they deserve will leave a good lasting impression of yourself. In Chinese business culture, humility is an important asset. Never exaggerate or be aggressive in making your point, as all of this will be regarded with doubt, and, in most cases, your claims will be investigated, or you will just lose the respect and attention you so worked hard to gain from your counterparts.

During a meeting people often keep business cards in front of them on the table to remind themselves of who's who – putting them away can be seen as impolite. The Chinese are very keen about exchanging business cards, so be sure to bring a plentiful supply. Ensure that one side is in English and the other is in Chinese, preferably in the local dialect.

If you are a key decision maker or in another senior position, then it is in your best interests to have your professional title listed on your business card. In Chinese culture, the main reason that business cards are exchanged is to determine who will be the key decision-makers on each side. You will then be able to gain the respect of that particular person throughout the talks. It's all part of the process of building a solid relationship and trust between the two parties.

In agreement with the cultural aspects of Chinese business procedures, it is normally anticipated that the delegation will enter the meeting room in a hierarchical order. For example, the Chinese will presume that the first person to enter the meeting room is the head of the visiting delegation.

Maintaining steady eye contact with your counterparts is a good sign in business – constantly looking away from the person you are talking to will give the impression that you are being rude and are not interested in the meeting. It can also make your interlocutor lose trust in you. In the west it is different; too much eye contact can make you and the other person feel uncomfortable. Since hierarchy is highly important in Chinese corporate culture, if you are not yourself a senior member of your organization then it is well worth bringing someone in a more senior position to lead the negotiations on your behalf. The Chinese side will do the same.

In the event that your colleagues find it difficult to pronounce your name, then most likely that you will be provided with a Chinese name – normally chosen by your colleagues. Sometimes you are given a number of Chinese names to choose from. It's a good thing because if you are a salesman constantly in contact with Chinese clients, it saves them the hassle of pronouncing your English name! In return your friends and colleagues may ask you to give them a good English name (see chapter on Chinese Names).

Most corporate executives tend to keep an album for their business cards, and in time you may end up with quite a number of albums as I noticed from personal

4

experience! Having a business card collection is very useful for the purposes of guangxi. When you want to look for a business opportunity or a new job then you can always flick through your album to find contacts that may be of assistance to you.

Business meals

A Business lunch is normally taken within the time frame that is allocated by the company for a lunch break. Business dinners however, tend to take much longer because there is no need for anyone to go back to the office. Employees usually sit with their colleagues rather than according to which department they belong to. Meals are formal events for most business people.

Formal dinners

During formal dinners and events the senior management will commence by making a short speech thanking colleagues for their hard work and wishing everyone a good week ahead (or whatever the occasion may be) and then go around making toasts with every employee. Normally non-managerial employees don't make a speech; however exceptions may be made to welcome new foreign employees to the company for example. If you are asked to make a speech then it is best to keep it short and snappy and offer plenty of thanks to your colleagues and your senior management. It is a way of maintaining respect and trust between yourself and the other members of your company.

Toasts

Just like in the West, where people give a toast to each other by touching glasses and saying 'Cheers!', in China there is a similar tradition, however with a little bit more energy! The Chinese equivalent of saying 'Cheers!' is 'Gambei!' (Pronounced Gam Bye) and during formal dinners, the senior manager or director goes around the tables and gives a toast to everyone with many shouts of 'Gambei!' – sometimes this is also done by everyone tapping the table with their glasses and then shouting 'Gambei!'. It's quite an experience to observe all of this joy as everyone lets off steam after a long day at work. When placing your chopsticks on the table during any meal (formal or not), it is best to avoid putting them facing downwards into a bowl of rice, as this is a symbol of death. Normally a chopstick stand is placed next to each dish for each person.

Avoid mentioning political terms such as 'Red China', 'Communist China' or making jokes about politically sensitive issues such as Taiwan or Tibet. Also avoid making any jokes about sex or using sarcasm with colleagues, unless they are very close to you and they understand your way of joking – otherwise you can find yourself in some embarrassing situations! The sense of humour of Westerners is very different from the Chinese sense of humour. While sitting with Chinese colleagues it is nice to talk about the weather, life in your homeland and how it is different from China, Chinese art and beautiful scenery and generally anything positive about China and your experiences there.

4

Political correctness

Bathrooms and toilets

Usually the public toilets are Asian style and most have very little, if any, privacy! Toilets in most multinational corporations are Western style, but the sewage system is not good, so toilets often get blocked. Unfortunately this can happen even in 5-star hotels.

All good hotels in China are equipped with a shower that has hot and cold water. Some hotels may also have a bathtub, but not always.

It is advisable that you always carry tissues with you at all times when in China as most public toilets (even in buildings which house multinational companies) have no tissue paper available. Also you may find it rather unhygienic that the majority of Chinese people prefer to throw the used tissue paper straight into the bin rather than flush it down the toilet. This is purely because the sewage system is not good and can easily get blocked. It also explains why tissue paper in China is perfumed.

Holidays

Chinese festivals are split according to either the solar calendar or the lunar calendar. There are nine holidays according to the solar calendar, while there are only five official holidays according to the lunar calendar.

4

Christmas Day in China is no different from any other day, as it is not officially celebrated here – but foreign hotels and multinational corporations will usually have a Christmas tree in the foyer along with a Santa Claus.

During the official Chinese holidays, streets are decorated with the national flags and special entertainments are organised in cities, where famous singers and actors mingle with the crowds and promote a sense of nationalism. Crowds are encouraged to participate in the singing of Patriotic songs, as well as traditional songs that tell stories about village life and the struggles during the Cultural Revolution.

Chinese New Year (Chun Jie)

Chinese New Year (known as the Spring Festival) usually falls towards the beginning of February or the end January. It is China's equivalent to the western Christmas period. The official holiday is for three days but people normally take extended leave for 7 days or even two weeks. After the holiday some people work for seven days in a row, thereby making up the two extra that were taken off.

For the holiday period of three days (it may as mentioned extend for a longer period), China is closed for business, as banks, law courts, and other government offices take a break.

It would not be a good idea to visit the week before Chinese New Year or in the two weeks afterwards, in case the person/s you have come to meet are on extended leave during that period.

In the weeks before the start of the Chinese New Year, streets, shops, homes and offices are decorated with red lights in the shape of Chinese lanterns, the legendary monkey king or other things associated with Chinese culture. People put up red and yellow coloured decorations on their front doors and inside the house to bring good luck for the coming year. Loud firecrackers are lit, in the belief that they will scare away evil spirits and bad luck.

4

Qing Ming festival

This is on the 3rd Month of the Chinese calendar. It's a day when people visit cemeteries and burial sites to pay respects to their ancestors.

October mid autumn festival (Zhong Qiu Jie)

Also known as the Golden week holiday or the Moon festival, the mid autumn festival is a time when people get to eat lots of delicious moon cakes. These are round cakes made with the standard ingredients wheat, sugar, and one or two dried egg yolks. Other moon cakes come with a variety of stuffings, according to the area of China in which they are sold. Varieties include dried fruit, nuts and meat (usually ham, duck or chicken). The legend goes that you should climb your nearest hill or mountain late in the evening to admire the full moon and eat moon cakes with friends, family or your loved one.

Rather expensive in some places, these cakes can be an ideal gift for anyone. Foreigners often find them very heavy and they can easily make you fat.

May Day

May Day falls on the 1st of May. There is not much public celebration of any sort; however the three-day official break from the office is welcome news.

Dragon boat festival

Apart from Chinese New Year, the Dragon boat festival, known as the 'Duan Wu Jie', is perhaps the best-known traditional Chinese festival. It falls on the fifth day of the fifth lunar month. The highlight of the festival is a race between rival teams on their local river in slim wooden boats in the shape of a dragon (usually with the front part representing the Dragon's face and the back part in the shape of a tail). Each team may have up to 8 contestants, all dressed in colourful traditional costumes and chanting patriotic songs to the beat of drums in the background.

On the riverbanks, shops sell boiled rice (known as 'Zhongzhi') mixed with vegetables or meat and wrapped in a banana leaf, made in the shape of a pyramid (known as 'Ketupat' in some parts of SE Asia such as Malaysia and Brunei).

4

The festival is said to commemorate the death of a minister and great poet of the State of Chu (Qu Yuan) during the Warring States Period (475-221 BC), who, according to legend, drowned himself in the river in protest after learning that his king did not accept his advice. To avoid sea life consuming his body, the people of Chu launched their boats and threw rice dumplings wrapped in bamboo leaves into the river where he drowned to feed the fish.

It's a very colourful event in cities such as Shanghai, Guangzhou and Hong Kong, where people line up on the banks of the rivers and cheer on the contestants. At the end of the race, in a gesture of good humour, the captain of the winning team is jubilantly thrown into the river by his team-mates before collecting the trophy from the mayor of the city.

What kind of gift to give?

Gifts should be given to your colleagues and friends according to their age and gender, just as you would do anywhere else in the world. There are a few exceptions in China. While young Chinese ladies would love to have the latest designer perfume, you should avoid giving a candles or a strong perfume to any lady who is above middle age ('Dior Poison' is out of the question here!), and instead a box of milk chocolates or any bath set with Lavender coloured or scented toiletries would make her smile! Red or gold coloured wrapping paper is a good choice, as these colours signify prosperity and fortune. For men and boys, a tie and shirt would be just fine, as well as bottle of nice wine or whiskey. For children toys are acceptable. Avoid giving anyone a green hat or any white flowers other than roses (Mao hats were green, and white flowers signify death!). It would be best to avoid giving a clock or watch to anyone as a gift, as this also represents death in Chinese culture! If you do by any chance end up giving such a gift by mistake, then don't worry, as a foreigner it is unlikely that you will lose friends over it. The worst case scenario would be losing a good negotiation by accidentally giving someone a clock on your last day in China!

Public holidays

The Chinese have the Lunar Calendar and in Hong Kong they have the Georgian Calendar but observe the Lunar dates as well. They get the best of both world's when it comes to public holidays!

Lunar New Year's Day (Chun Jie): This coincides with the New Moon in late January/Early February for 3 days (Hong Kong and China).

International Working Women's Day: March 8th. Celebrated in China only.

Qing Ming Jie: Usually on 4th or 5th April (Hong Kong and China).

Good Friday: The Friday before Easter Sunday – usually in the 2nd or 3rd week of April. Celebrated in Hong Kong Only.

Easter Monday: Usually in the 2nd or 3rd week of April (Hong Kong only).

Labour Day: 1st May – (China and Hong Kong).

Chinese Youth Day: 4th May (China and Hong Kong).

Buddha's Birthday: Eighth day of the fourth moon (Chinese calendar) – (Hong Kong only).

International Children Day's: September 10th – (China only).

Duan Wu Jie (Dragon Boat Festival): Known as Tuen Ng Festival in Hong Kong – it's on the fifth day of the fifth lunar month (China and Hong Kong).

Hong Kong Special Administrative Region Establishment Day: 1st July (Hong Kong only).

Army Day: 1st August – (China only).

Mid Autumn Festival: 15th day of 8th lunar month – usually in the 3rd or 4th week of September.

4

4

Day following the Mid-Autumn Festival: Sixteenth day of the eighth moon (Chinese calendar). Hong Kong and China.

National Day: 1st October for three days (China and Hong Kong).

Chung Yeung Festival: Ninth day of the ninth moon (Chinese calendar) – usually October

Christmas and Boxing day: 25th and 26th December – (Hong Kong only).

getting down
to business

getting down to business

This chapter provides elementary guidance on the etiquette of business, and also contains details of useful local organisations who can assist with the more complicated requirements of business transactions.

Why China?

In a nutshell, the simplest answer to this question is that when China opened its door to the outside world in the early 1980s, people were finally given an opportunity to invest in a market that had been closed for so many years. Before the market reforms instigated by Deng Xiaoping (1904–1997), China had been closed for business (just like North Korea is today). Now people (both Chinese and foreigners) are taking advantage of the openness of the Chinese economy by investing, and by promoting goods and services that the rest of the world has enjoyed for many years but are still relatively new to China. Other factors, such as the country's sheer size – both geographically and in terms of population – also contributed to the remarkable success of China's economy in recent years.

China has become in recent years one of the top three trading partners of the US, UK, Australia, France and other countries. The crash of the Asian economies in 1997 had a serious knock-on effect on many economies but China maintained a powerful attraction for foreign investors. Even during unfortunate events such as the 9/11 attacks in 2001, the SARS epidemic in 2003 and the Asian Tsunami in 2004, China has stayed strong and, amazingly, managed to brush aside these events to keep its annual GDP growth up, from an average of about 7.3 per cent in 2001 to approximately 10.9 per cent in 2008. It has remained around 10 per cent for the past six years.

After fifteen years as a guest member, China's membership of the WTO formerly known as GATT was finally cemented in December 2001. The admission to the WTO has been a significant factor in the growth of foreign investment in major cities in China and has made it easier for less well-known Chinese companies to expand overseas. Cities like Shanghai and Shenzhen are increasingly being seen as the new 'Hong Kong' of the mainland.

WTO

Countries wishing to trade with China or compete with China, in terms of imports and exports to the European or SE Asian markets, are eager not to permit too much appreciation of their own currencies against

5

5

the Renmenbi. When China lets the Renmenbi appreciate at a steady pace, other countries are not in a position to allow quick appreciation of their respective currencies. Just as the percentage of imports and exports to countries in Europe and North America has increased, so has the control of the Chinese exchange rate strategy on those currencies. As mentioned earlier, China eventually decided to increase the appreciation by only about ten per cent since July 2005 – this is great news if you are a property investor or a corporate director wanting to get that much-needed business start up, but most economists argue that it is not enough of an appreciation and there is no set prediction as to how long it will remain at this rate. The Renmenbi's value in November of 2008 was approximately 6.90 RMB/USD. Originally it was pegged at around 8.28 RMB/USD in July 2005.

In the 1980s and 1990s, everyone had Russia, Japan and Korea on their list of countries to make friends with. Nobody really forecasted or imagined that, come the year 2000, we would all be turning our attention to Asia's two biggest giants, namely India and China. Now what do we see? In just seven years (since 2000 and the famous Y2K computer glitch), foreign multinationals are outsourcing their manufacturing and Research and Design facilities to China because of low cost labor and cheaper land to invest in initially.

Brainstorming

If you are really eager to enter the land of the dragon, then it's always best to get as much advice as possible from friends, colleagues and organisations (some of which are listed in Chapter 2). Do your research thoroughly because once you are in China, it is a make or break time; no business corporation can afford to get trapped in a situation where they have established a business but don't know where to go from there. Here are some questions that you should ask yourself beforehand as you gather all the information:

1. Am I prepared for the long haul?
2. Does my business have enough surpluses in case we are not successful in setting up a business in China?

3.   More importantly – following on from Question
      2 – Can I/we afford to afford to invest in China,
      Hong Kong or Macau?
4.   Do I have the right employees who I know can
      manage my office in China?
5.   How long am I, or the shareholders, prepared
      to wait before we see any financial return on
      the investment?
6.   What about Intellectual Property rights?
      (more about this later in the chapter)
7.   Am I aware of all the legal issues concerned
      with China?
8.   Am I/we aware of the tax issues concerned
      with importing/exporting goods out of China?
9.   What would be the best location for our
      business? Why? Would we face direct
      competition from local/multinationals?

5

Advantages and disadvantages of the China market

There are myriad consultancies that offer a whole range
of reasons for and against setting up in China. I will
not go into all of them as that is not in the scope of
this book. However, here are a few selected reasons
from my own personal experience in China as to why
companies may find it beneficial, and what challenges
they may face when starting out in China:

Advantages:

Cost of labor

Everyone now knows in the business world that if you
were to hire an Engineer in the USA with, say, ten years
of really good experience under their belt, it would cost
you roughly US$90,000 per annum plus any substantial
benefits; however, hire the same person, with the same
skills in China, and you may be looking at paying them
approximately 10,000 RMB per month (approximately
US$18,000 per annum). This can save a substantial
amount if you are hiring in bulk and investing in a
large workforce.

5

Educated workforce and scale

According to the 2007 figures from the United Nations Development Programme, China has a literacy rate of over 90 per cent, and in 2007 produced over 20 million graduates – that's almost 3 per cent of the population and more than any other country in the world. Education is of great importance in Chinese culture and it is those 20 million graduates that will be responsible for the great future of this country.

Domestic market attraction and growth (SEZ)

Over past three decades a number of Special Economic Zones (SEZs) have been established for the purpose of encouraging trade and an area where private enterprises as well as multinationals can set up businesses. Shenzhen was the first to be introduced in 1979 and around the same time four other cities were introduced.

Achievements of these SEZs, particularly Shenzhen and Pudong (Shanghai) have been used as examples for other cities in China to follow. For foreign investment, both the Pearl River Delta and the Yangtze River Delta became two powerful areas that have continued to fuel the country's growing economy.

Olympics

Beijing 2008

The Olympic Games are always seen as an opportunity to promote the culture, ethics and business prospects of countries that have the privilege to host them. The Beijing 2008 Olympics, which China worked so hard to prepare for, was an opportunity for multinationals and Chinese companies to grow in China, and build economic connections. A large amount of economic growth was predicted after the Olympics finished, and this will no doubt include outsourcing and inward investment for foreign and local SMEs as well as multinationals.

Disadvantages:

English language and communications skills

In spite of the advantages of an educated workforce mentioned earlier, on the whole when doing business in most parts of China, language is still a major problem. This will no doubt improve in years ahead.

High import/export taxation or duties

The laws regarding taxation of goods in China are strict and the tax rates are high (as much as 70 per cent tax on some products). If you have your own trading business, and you want to import or export goods from China, then your best bet is to first find out as much as you can about the relevant tax laws from a good financial consultant or from your own country's trade department. For the UK, the Trade & Investment department would be the best way forward (www.uktradeinvest.gov.uk). For the US check the website (www.export.gov/china).

The regulations regarding importing and exporting of goods can change without notice, so it is best to check with your shipping agents for the latest information. In Hong Kong on the other hand there is no exchange control and very few or no trade restrictions – it is a free trading port. For further information on import and export laws, issues and other up to date news, please check Croner's Reference Book for Exporters (www.croners.co.uk). As of 2007, China also has dual taxation agreements with 78 countries, including the UK and the US. Further details may be found from China's Ministry of Taxation website: www.chinatax.gov.cn

Cultural challenges in the office

For most foreign corporations, it's not just the language problems that will need to be tackled; it is also the local culture. No matter how good your language skills, for foreigners it will always be challenging to fit into the culture, whether this be at work or in personal life.

Other disadvantages include the following:

Decisions all made by just the senior management
Limited number of International Name Brands
Limited amount of International exposure and experience (not like Hong Kong)
Risk of Intellectual Property being lost (more about this later in the chapter)
Limited Marketing and Selling Skills by corporations
Shortage of Mid-Top-End Skilled Professionals and Management (very hierarchical – this is not the way to do International business)

5

While it seems like the disadvantages outweigh the advantages, you shouldn't be discouraged. The disadvantages can be overcome in time and even made into advantages (such as language skills for example). Entering China as a prospective business may be difficult, but it is not impossible!

No problem!

You will hear this phrase in meetings, negotiations and anywhere there is a general feel that a problem will exist. Because losing face in China is very big thing most people will give the impression that everything is fine! In Mandarin the pronunciation is in two forms as: 'May wen tee!' or 'May guan xi!', whereas in Cantonese it is pronounced: 'Mo man tai!'

Channels into the China market

There are several approaches one can take, in order to enter the Chinese market.

I will describe three main routes and then give some examples of cost effective ways to go about them (as some can be very expensive):

The Hong Kong approach:

For those not familiar with China, it may be beneficial for your business to be set up in Hong Kong for quite some time before opening an office on the mainland. There are a whole host of advantages in doing this, but the main drawback here is that in Hong Kong you are not exposed to the 'real' Chinese market, culture or even language. Hong Kong is more international than the mainland; the working language is Cantonese and not Mandarin; renting an office is expensive; Legal & Tax issues are different; and the general way of working and living is different from mainland China. In Hong Kong there are no obstacles to market entry, and money from Hong Kong can be easily repatriated.

The Mainland China approach:

This is for the more adventurous minded business executive. This will involve a gamble. If you want to jump straight into the China pool, and set up an office in, say, Shanghai (where most foreign companies head when they first come to China), the challenges will be greater but of course if you overcome them, the rewards can be greater too. You may want to appoint a western educated, Chinese manager to take care of your office in China – that way you will have peace of mind knowing that someone who understands the culture and principles of China, as well as western business mindsets, is able to take care of the day to day running of your business without you worrying too much. This saves the costs of using a Management consultancy.

5

The Management Consultancy route:
The downside to the above approaches is that as a manager based remotely in Europe or America you will never be totally in control of the day to day business in your Hong Kong or China office. This means that remotely based managers need to rely entirely upon the honesty of their locally based business partner or management level staff members. So to make things easier and provide a more hassle free option, using a management consultancy could be the appropriate answer. This may prove most beneficial as your risk is lowered and you are guided into the correct path all the way through – right from the conception phase of your project to the business fulfilment stage – but it is also the most expensive route. You will have to do your research to find the right consultancy and then discuss the appropriate options with them. A list of some well-known consultancies is provided in Chapter 2.

When looking at the above three approaches, you may want to adopt any of the following options:

Appointing a representative company
Companies that take this approach sometimes use the word 'reseller' to describe representative companies. This is by far the simplest method and will give you the least problems. All that needs to be done is to sign an agreement and a memorandum of understanding to confirm that you are appointing a company that will represent you on the market. They will agree to sell your product based on your lowest price, to which they will add a certain margin for themselves. Your reseller will negotiate with you the correct purchase price for products, and you will then transfer the difference, as commission to the representative's account.

5

Working with an agent or distributor

An agent works on a similar basis as a 'representative company', but the agent will fund the transaction and in the process, disguise his margin on the deal. A distributor (or 'disti' as they are known in the trade for short), will normally keep your products for re-selling to the market through their own network. When dealing with a distributor, it's important that secure payments of goods are made, as some of their clients will be provided with extended credit, so therefore you could find yourself in a situation where you will have to pay, only when you receive payment.

The more expensive route

In accordance with China's foreign investment laws, investment ventures commonly used in China are China-foreign Equity Joint Ventures (EJV); Co-operative (or contractual) Joint Ventures (CJV); Wholly Foreign-Owned Enterprises (WFOE); Joint Stock Companies; China Holding Companies (CHC); Representative Offices (RO); Assembling and Processing Contracts (APC), and branches. From these, here are a few more details for some of them:

Setting up a Joint Venture (JV)

Historically many **Foreign Invested Enterprises** (**FIE**) are set up as **Joint Ventures** (**JV**) and for certain industries, MOFTEC approval would normally only be granted to JVs. FIEs can also be set up as Wholly Foreign Owned Enterprises (WFOE).

Two types of JVs exist, an Equity Joint Venture (EJV) and a Contractual or Co-operative Joint Venture (CJV). An EJV is a limited liability corporation and a legal entity in China. Partners jointly operate the EJV; share the risks, profits and losses according to their share of the equity. Foreign partners are allowed to repatriate their share.

CJVs works slightly differently to EJVs. Under the CJV, the Chinese partner will provide the JV with non-liquid assets, e.g., land, energy resources, labour, usable buildings, machinery and facilities etc. Capital, technology, materials and so on will be provided by the foreign partners. A CVJ contract is signed, detailing the rights and the obligations of each party, and also the distribution of the CJV's products, revenues and profits. These profits are shared in accordance with the proportions stipulated in the contract agreement.

In some recent cases, there have been examples where JVs are being converted into WFOEs by the FIEs because there have been some conflicts of interest, and as an effect of these conflicts some Chinese partners have filed official complaints with the tax authority of the other parties' ministries about any alleged violation by the foreign investors.

5

Establishing your own company (WFOE)

A Wholly Foreign Owned Enterprises (WFOE) is an enterprise established in China that has its entire capital fully invested by foreign interests. WFOEs operate under Chinese law, and are expected by their foreign investors to actively generate high profits and fuel China's economy, and yield taxation revenues for the Chinese government. WFOEs are normally not your average sized SMEs.

China Holding Company (CHC)

This is probably the most expensive option, and one that most multinational corporations are willing to consider as part of their expansion plans. To be able to set up a CHC, there is a requirement for corporations to have at least US$30 million, and to add to the constraints, it has to be fully paid up within two years – which shouldn't be a problem for your average global corporation – but (and it's a big but!) there are also significant amounts of tax and other operational costs involved. The CHC has been successfully implemented by many of the well established corporation in China including Coca-Cola, IMB-Lenovo (Lenovo is China's number one PC Manufacturer), Siemens, Sony, Danone, Boeing and General Electric to name just a few.

As of the end of 2007, fourteen of the twenty foreign semiconductor firms in China have set up a CHC. Location wise, it is interesting to know that in 2008 over ninety-four per cent of the CHCs were based in Shanghai, Beijing and Shenzhen. CHCs provide multinationals with the exposure that they may not otherwise be able to achieve on their own in China. Qualifying CHCs who want to restructure their operations or improve their presence in the market can sell anywhere in the world!

Setting up a Joint Development (JD)

Joint Development is less used by corporations onshore; it's more for the Oil and Gas industries, and mainly offshore accounts. Its best to get more advice about JDs from a good management consultancy, simply because of the complexities involved.

Establishing a Compensation Trade (Counter Trade)

This involves joint control over the venture, with the Chinese partner normally providing the buildings and labour force, and the foreign partner providing all the necessary technology, supervision and advice on the business as a whole. Again expert advice from a consultant should be sought if you serious about going ahead with this venture.

Buying a local Chinese company and incorporating their operations with yours.

If you are a local Chinese private sector company, then this may be a better option for you to consider. It is difficult for a foreign corporation to buy or invest in a public sector corporation.

The smallest amount of registered capital needed for Foreign Investment Enterprise (FIE) varies between corporations. According to 'the global Administration Measure for Foreign Investment in Commercial Sector', the amount of registered capital needed has been substantially reduced. For example, in 2007 the minimum registered capital requirement for a wholesaling enterprise was approximately RMB 500,000 (about US$67,568) and for a retailing enterprise it was roughly RMB 300,000 (approx US$40,541). In accordance with the 'Company Law' of mainland China, any limited liability company's registered capital shall not be less than the listed amount as follows (highly unlikely that it will change dramatically for a few years):

Operation of Limited company	Capital Required RMB (USD) 2008 Figures
Companies engaging in production and operation	RMB 500,000 (US$67568)
Companies engaging in commercial wholesale	RMB 500,000 (US$67568)
Companies engaging in commercial retail	RMB 300,000 (US$40541)
Companies engaging in scientific and technological development and consulting service	RMB 100,000 (US$13514)
Companies limited by shares	RMB 10,000,000 (US$1351351)
Listed companies	RMB 50,000,000 (US$6756757)

Source: China Ministry of Information

Leasing Deal

Foreign companies usually provide the Chinese leaser with specific equipment (including any machinery), or any other services, either directly, or through a leasing corporation. This is very common with airline companies in China, where charter and private airlines wet-lease aircraft from either foreign airlines or from leasing companies such as Cabot Aviation (www.cabotaviation.com) who provide global airlines with leased aircraft.

It may be useful to contact companies such as PWC (www.pwc.com), Ernest & Young (www.ey.com) or KPMG (www.kpmg.com) for more detailed information on this subject.

Intellectual Property (IP)

As a foreign business that has never worked in China before, it would be very wise to protect your intellectual property rights, even before you set a single foot into the country. This is particularly important if you believe that your business idea or service is unique and is going to be a first on the Chinese mainland.

Knockoffs

Without being controversial or politically incorrect, it is fair to say that in China you can find a copy of almost any product or service that is branded in the western world. This is not an exaggeration; I will provide a few examples so that you get the picture. In Shenzhen's Dongmen area for example or the SEG Electronic Market near the Huaqiangbei area, I can guarantee you that in almost any store you will find high quality knock-offs; copies so good that it is almost impossible to tell the difference between fake and real products. This can include anything from designer Jeans to the latest Nintendo Wii games console. It is so common that the big corporations' products are sometimes outnumbered by these 'Made in Shenzhen or Guangzhou' products. In China, IP infringements don't only affect the industrial consumer products, but also the food or restaurant chains. For example there were legal issues with a Chinese coffee company that used the same brand logo as Starbucks and went by a slightly different name that would have got any consumer confused. Another example is drinks such as 'Red-Bull' – the whole packaging, including the size of the can and the brand logo – even the taste of the drink – is exactly the same as the real 'Red-Bull'. There are endless examples but I won't go in to every one.

Of course, China has all the essential laws in place (Copyright, Trademark and Patent laws), but it's only in recent years that the government has tried to clamp down on the copy culprits to resolve this serious problem. I was told by the Chinese manager at my former multinational that historically, Intellectual Property rights have always been something of a foreign custom to the Chinese culture because the Chinese like to share their ideas with each other. It was only when market reforms opened in 1979 that China formally acknowledged and protected Intellectual Property Rights (IPR) and in the following year China became a member of the World Intellectual Property Organization (WIPO), who are based in Geneva. The WIPO publish a monthly journal, *Industry Property*, which you may find useful.

WIPO

5

One of China's best Intellectual Property training centres offers world class IP training and materials to anyone interested in gaining more in-depth information about this field. The Beijing HQ, located in the Shangdi District of the capital, has hosted many important IP rights conferences for foreign countries, corporations as well as for those on trade missions. I was lucky enough to be invited by a good friend to an ASEAN organised conference held in the summer of 2006, which invited all the delegations from the main countries in the ASEAN (part of the SE Asian group of countries) region. The conference was chaired by UN officials as well as delegates from the Chinese government in charge of IP in China.

5

So what can you do to protect your IP right? Below are a few pointers:

- Be aware of the risks beforehand and get some sound advice from your country's own IPR organisation.
- Be aware of your potential partner in case they decide to leave the company; don't get paranoid but just be on the watch.
- Consult a lawyer specialising in IP matters on the mainland.
- Register your internet website domain name
- Read the regulations beforehand
- Maintain control and be careful of contributing your Intellectual Property.
- If you happen to see a store or product featuring your brand logo; and their company's name is just the direct Chinese translation of your company's name (this happened to KFC!), then consult your lawyer and the Chinese IP organisation.

The State Intellectual Property Office
www.sipo.gov.cn (English and Chinese)

Air and Sea Freight

Air freight
Polar Air Cargo, CargoLux, Focus Air Cargo and Atlas Air are just some of the many dedicated air freight

5

companies that fly into Chinese airports. Commercial airlines that have subsidiary cargo branches also offer freight services into Chinese cities. Air China Cargo, for example, is a freight subsidiary of the national flag carrier, Air China.

Airfreight is of course more expensive than sea freight, but less time consuming. In 2008, Shanghai Pudong airport alone handled more than four million tonnes of cargo, while Beijing and Guangzhou airports each handled just over 1.12 million tonnes.

China's 467 domestic and international registered airports together handled almost six million tonnes in 2008, with over 70 per cent for the international sector, and the rest in the domestic market.

Apart from well known companies like DHL (www.cn.dhl.com), UPS (www.ups.com) and Fedex (www.fedex.com), here are some more airfreight companies operating to China:
Air Bridge Cargo: www.airbridgecargo.com
Air China Cargo: www.airchina.com.cn
AHK Air Hong Kong Cargo:
www.airhongkong.com.hk
Atlas Air: www.atlasair.com
Cargolux Airlines: www.cargolux.com
Focus Air Cargo: www.focusaircargo.com
Great Wall Airlines: www.gwairlines.com
Jade Cargo: www.jadecargo.com
Polar Air Cargo: www.polaraircargo.com
Volga-Dnepr Airlines: www.volga-dnepr.com

Sea freight

P&O Shipping, Evergreen Shipping, China Shipping, OOCL and Maersk are just a few of the many well known shipping companies that operate in China's busy ports. The most common form of container (or Box) is either 20ft (6m) or 40ft (12m) and in 2008; over 400 million tonnes were shipped into and out of Hong Kong port (www.pdc.gov.hk). It is difficult to get accurate figures for Mainland China, simply because of the sheer size of the country and the large number of busy ports. Rough figures by economic analysts suggest that in 2008, over 4 billion tonnes of freight was shipped into and out of China's ports. By 2010, it is expected that over a third of the world's shipping would be handled from Chinese ports.

There are different kinds of container, ranging from the standard 'dry' unit, refrigerated units ('reefers') used for processed food, meat or fish products, open topped (for cars and other such products) and flat racks for transporting out of gauge equipment. The 'Payloads' can range from 22 tonnes anything up to 30 tonnes depending on the overall payload on a ship on a particular journey. Ships are checked by customs inspectors on a regular basis, especially if the ship arrives via a port that is popular with smugglers.

Containers

5

Some useful links for sea freight companies:
Maersk Container: www.maerskline.com
P&O Nedloyd Shipping: www.ponl.com
COSCO: www.cosco.com.cn
Evergreen Container: www.evergreen-marine.com
China Shipping: www.cnshipping.com
OOCL: www.oocl.com

Financing exports

This can be divided into long term and short term finance.

Short term finance

When dealing in international trade, especially with a emerging economy such as China, corporations need to be wary of the risks involved and need to assess the risks they are willing to take in order to be successful in that market. These risks can be, as mentioned in this chapter, IP related, Tax related or associated to other issues to do with import and export. There are also other serious financial risks (normally these are clearly laid out in the Terms & Conditions of any financial agreement between two parties):

- A **Credit risk** is a risk of alterations in the credit of an opposing business for the foreign company.
- An **Exchange risk** is one that is derived from alterations in the foreign exchange rate.
- A **Force majeure risk** is either a risk in trade

5

failure caused by an adjustment in a country's political or economic policy or a risk of natural disaster.

When negotiating on any price issues, there is always a dilemma when each party is waiting for the other to pay up first. In order for risks or any other misunderstandings to be limited between two parties, it is always best to have an official memorandum of understanding between the two negotiating parties. Banks and other export advisors will strongly recommend that payment should be secured using written confirmation on a 'Letter of Credit' (or LC or short). An LC is a normal way of obtaining payment. Basically it is a document issued by a financial institution which usually provides a binding payment to a recipient alongside any company terms and conditions as confirmed on the LC. The payment to your account will be transferred once the client has accepted the documents and settled on the resolution with the originating bank.

Payment can also be made using a Confirmed International Letter of Credit (CILC), which will be established with a bank in your native country. A CILC means that the bank will pay you irrespective of any problems in the originating country, provided you present all the documents to the bank. The payment period can be either 2 weeks, 30 days, 60 days, 90 days or 180 days; usually from the date on the Bill of Lading (A document issued by a Ship/Air/Road freight carrier).

Another useful payment method is the Cash Against Documents (CAD). A CAD is a transaction in which the buyer assumes the title for the products being purchased upon paying the auction price in cash. It is a mutual agreement and trust between you and the client whereby you give them an open credit to pay you.

Insurance against non-payment is available through Short Term Policies available from Gerling NCM Credit (www.gerling.com), and from the Euler Hermes group (www.eulerhermes.com), however, like all insurance companies there are costs, as well as each company's individual terms and conditions which will be attached to the cover letter.

One risk, which is very unlikely (although don't rule any possibilities out), is that some customers, when they are aware that you are insured against non-payment, will see it as an excuse for not paying you, knowing that you are covered.

Medium and long term finance

There are two major sources of medium to long term financial assistance to businesses investing in China.

Multilateral Aid

The World Bank (www. worldbankgroup.org) and the Asian Development Bank (www.adb.org) are the two main sources for these funds. They have the advantage that there is little or no interest on any repayments, and the term can be as long as possible. Of course this unlimited term can trap you into thinking that there is no rush to pay anything back. So you run the risk of continuing to churn out as much money as you can without realising that all the while you are building up more and more interest on your debt. But that is only if your financial plans go awry. Another disadvantage is that the Chinese Ministry of Finance only uses this for top priority projects, and in order to get approval from them, like anything else, can take a very long time.

Bilateral Aid

Government assisted and private Chinese banks can assist in providing funds. Although you would be much better off with the latter because there is not the same red tape and bureaucracy involved so the services are much quicker. China Merchants Bank (www.cmbchina.com) is the largest and most popular private bank on the mainland. Banks in your own country will also be able to assist. The supplier can have peace of mind that their payments will be delivered on time, usually within 30 days from the receipt of required documents. The only major disadvantage is that the aid is strictly controlled, and the terms and conditions are stringent and depend on the type of project for which the aid is intended.

5

5

Choosing a location in China

Locating your business in China for the first time can be a daunting task for any foreign corporation. It seems at first glance that no matter where you set up your business, you will make a profit, provided of course you do it logically. Some important factors which you should take into account are: climate, transport accessibility and how welcoming the region is to foreign investors? You must also ask yourself if the market for your product/s exists in that particular part of China?

Of course it's all about long term stability, profit, and peace of mind when you are 6000 miles away from the office!

East Coast

Economic maps indicate that the majority of China's industry is located on the East Coast. There are a number of reasons for this, the obvious one being the easy access to shipping ports such as Shanghai, Tianjin, Dalian, Shenzhen, Xiamen and Guangzhou. Another reason is competition – if one company has established a business in Shanghai, then it makes sense for their competitors to relocate there as well.

The 'Shanghai Vision' has been in place for a few years and its aim is to put the city at the centre of the International business world's attention and make it a world class city by 2015, and also to increase GDP by over 15 per cent by the same year. Shanghai will also host the much anticipated 2010 Expo. The Pudong area of Shanghai is one of the fastest growing regions in the world, with new high rise office buildings and luxury apartments going up every year.

The **Shanghai IFC (International Finance Centre)** is managed by the famous Sun Kung Hai Properties (www.shkp.com, who are also behind Hong Kong's tallest building, Two IFC Tower, and many other property projects in Shanghai), and is set to be one of the world's tallest buildings at approximatly 260m when it opens in 2009. HSBC will occupy thirty stories of the building and it will be appropriately named the 'HSBC Building-Shanghai IFC'.

5

This East coast region will bring in more investment into areas such as IT, Real Estate, Financial Services, the Automobile industry, the Aviation industry, Semiconductors and Telecommunications.

Just to the north of Shanghai and Suzhou in Jiangsu Province is **Wuxi** (pronounced Wu Shee, www.wuxi.gov.cn), which has an average annual GDP of around RMB 376 billion (as of 2007) and a population of only around 5 million. It is home to foreign multinationals such as: Timken, Infineon Technologies, Agfa and Sharp among others. More information can be found from the **Wuxi Bureau of Foreign Trade and Economic corporation** – (www.wxmofcom.gov.cn).

Special Economic Zones (SEZ)

An obvious choice may well be any of the SEZs that have opened up since 1979. The latest addition has been the twin city SEZ of Chongqing-Chengdu as described in chapter ten. More information about SEZs is provided in chapter seven. In the SEZs, there are no licenses or quotas required (except for passive quotas) and privileged handling of import duty and import-associated taxes is offered. SEZs are listed independently by nationwide planning (including financial planning) and have province-level authority on economic management.

SEZ

All trade and commercial activities undertaken between enterprises within SEZs and enterprises outside the zones (but within mainland China) are regarded as foreign trade, and the usual import and export rules & regulations apply.

The benefits of setting up a business in a Special Economic Zone (SEZ):

1.   Special tax incentives for foreign investments in the SEZs.
2.   Greater independence on international trade activities.
3.   Economic characteristics are represented as '3 principles' of SEZs:
      A.   Creation of SEZs usually relies on attracting and utilizing foreign capital

B. Primary economic forms are sino-foreign JVs and partnerships as well as Wholly Foreign-Owned Enterprises (WFOE)
C. Products are primarily export-oriented

South China: The Pearl River Delta (PRD)

Even though Shanghai and Beijing are two major Chinese cities that are always at the centre of the world's attention (and will continue to change China's economy dramatically in the next ten to fifteen years) foreign investors must bear in mind that China's most prosperous cities are actually situated in the southern province of Guangdong. Guangdong province was the region where (in Shenzhen), Deng Xiaoping, opened the market and trade zones to the outside world, with China's first four Special Economic Zones. Much of that development has been fueled by the region's proximity to Hong Kong, Macau and the rest of south-east Asia.

The 'Pearl River Delta' or PRD, consists of Guangdong plus the Special Administrative Regions (SAR) of Hong Kong and Macau. Cities that should be on your 'must go' business trip include: Hong Kong, Zhuhai, Shenzhen, Guangzhou, Foshan, Xhongshan, Macau and Haikou.

It is amazing when one is presented with figures that suggest that Guangdong province might on its own have a manufacturing workforce larger than that of America. Guangdong's population is over 85 million people (2007 statistics). If even one fifth of its population held a manufacturing job, approximately 18 million, that would completely outnumber America's entire Manufacturing sector, which employees just over 15 million. It is an eye-opener and the reason you see so many American and European companies jumping at the first opportunity to establish a presence in Guangdong Province.

Zhuhai (www.zhuhai.gov.cn) has been another success story for the Special Economic Zone in Guangdong Province with an annual GDP of around RMB 65 billion in 2007. It borders the SAR of Macau, and although it does not get as much attention as Shenzhen does (partly as a result of its bordering Hong Kong), Zhuhai still manages to accommodate an abundance of industries (mainly Electrical equipment, Petrochemicals and

5

Medical equipment) that would make any foreign investors flock to this city.

Some useful Zhuhai websites:
Zhuhai Foreign Trade and Economic Cooperation Bureau
www.zhuhai-trade.gov.cn

Zhuhai Foreign Investment Service Centre
www.zhuhai.com.cn

5

Western China
Chapter nine talks about Chongqing, the largest and most populated province in China with over 32 million people, becoming one of the leading provinces in China's economic boom. Chongqing is situated on the upper reaches of the famous Yangtze River, and is the only Municipality in south-west China which reports directly to the government. The city has a booming airport (Jiangbei Airport), which in 2007 served almost 7 million passengers. Chongqing is also home to Asia's largest aluminum plant, the South West Aluminum plant, which rolled out over 300,000 tonnes of finished products in 2007. In 2007, Chongqing had a GDP of almost 348.6 billion RMB. Other areas of interest for foreign investors in the western China regions may include:

- **Oil and Gas Sector**
- **Aerospace**
- **Semiconductor and Electronics Industry**
- **Steel**
- **Construction Materials**
- **The ongoing development of the Metro system in Chongqing** (one operational line at the moment).

VAT refund for exporters
Normally the only people in the authority to reclaim VAT (Value Added Tax usually set at 17.5 per cent) are exporters or suppliers for certain tender projects that are financed by international financial institutions (e.g. World Bank (www.worldbank.org) or the International Monetary Fund (www.imf.org). As mentioned that the standard VAT rate is set at 17 per cent, this excludes some products (e.g. cereal and edible vegetable oils, books, tap water, heaters, liquefied petroleum gas,

5

natural gas, biogas and coal products for suburban use) whose import is set at a standard VAT rate of 13 per cent. VAT cannot be reclaimed by every exporter; factors that decide if a business is eligible to reclaim VAT include but not limited to:

- The type of products they supply or export
- Businesses that supply to Government-labeled categories (Machinery like sewing equipment or electronic products)

Reclaiming VAT is not as straight forward a process as one would like, and for advice it is best to get in touch with a Chamber of Commerce, a good financial consultant or the relevant Trade & Investment department in your country.

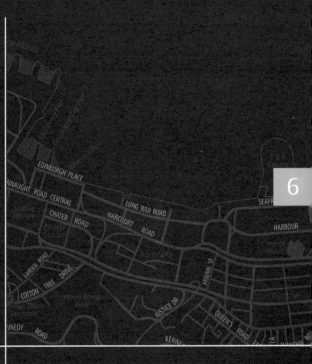

6

major industries

major industries

This is an overview of each
of the major industries of
the nation, and where they
stand today

'Made in China'

China's economic growth in recent years is nothing short of a miracle and is continually seen as a role model by other developing nations around the world. Of course much attention is also given to other emerging powerhouses such as India, Brazil and Mexico – but China is a step ahead.

Aircraft parts, agricultural products and machinery, forest products, high-tech equipment, textiles, automotive industry and seafood are among China's top export commodities to foreign economies. In return foreign investors make use of Chinese land, labor, infrastructure, knowledge and technology to help with their business needs and services to the world. Multinational corporations and globally respected brands such as Boeing, Airbus, Starbucks, MacDonald's, Range Rover, Mercedes Benz, Pizza Hut, as well as countless smaller companies, have significant business presence in China. Altogether there are over 37 industries in China, Hong Kong and Macau.

Just going around your local departmental store in Europe or America, it is interesting to see the number of goods labeled 'Made in China'. In the 1980s the buzz word in the electrical industry was 'Made in Taiwan', or 'Japan', with a few exceptions for locally made products in the West. The impact that China's growth has made has been quite an eye-opener. I ended up in China in 2003 due to a mixture of persuasion and just being in the right place at the right time. One of my friend's came back from a holiday in the US and she said 'Almost everything in the States says "Made in China". There are a few products that say "Proudly Made in the USA", but other than that most furniture, materials, paints, and even food says "Produce of China".' She went on to say that I should go to China to take a look for myself.

Her initial comments were 'They are building large dual carriageways on top of each other. In London you have Canary Wharf; I guarantee that in one normal city in China you will see at least five Canary Wharfs!'. Her comments might have sounded as if she was exaggerating at first, but she was not, as I realised on

6

Foreign investment

my first trip to this country. You really have to see it to be able to believe it. I feel privileged to witness this growth.

China should not be a seen as the 'World's Sweatshop Capital' or a Manufacturer of cheap and bad quality goods, as many economists used to say in the 1990s. On my first trip to factories around the Dongguan area, I was expecting to find people working long hours without breaks, cramped into hot and dark rooms by their managers – but I was horribly wrong. China should not be seen as a country where labor is exploited for the benefit of multinationals. These days most companies have staff just as professional and organised as any company in the West. The Chinese government has also set international standards to be met, including requiring managers to treat their workers fairly. The Chinese are a very intelligent people, built on a culture that encourages hard work and entrepreneurship.

It is part of the culture that if you don't succeed at school or in the office, then not only are you letting yourself down, but consequently you lose face with friends and family because everyone will think that you are either lazy or not determined enough. Where we see China now is just the tip of the iceberg. This country and its people have a great deal to offer for the future.

A good question to ask is: what if investment in this emerging nation results in the unlikely situation of 'too many eggs in one basket', where China becomes such an important and powerful nation of manufacturers, that it could hold the rest of the world to ransom with the supply and prices of its goods? It is an extreemly unlikely situation but it would make it difficult for the rest of the world to refuse to buy from China.

A great country is one, whose government encourages the manufacture and export of good quality products and services required by the world, at a fraction of the cost it would take other economies to produce, and in return is able to attract and generate foreign exchange. China does all of this beautifully.

For China to expand its base it has to attract Foreign Direct investment (FDI), and in October of 2008, it was

International
standards

reported that China built up US$62 billion in FDI in the year, an increase of almost eleven per cent on the first half of 2006.

Bicycle – a dying Breed?

It would have seemed a joke to Mao Zedong if a Chinese fortune teller had told him that by 2008, there would be more planes and automobiles in China than any other country in the world; and that the bicycle would be a dying breed! However, in Beijing, thankfully there are still signs that the tradition is not dying out altogether. When I went to Beijing, in 2007, one of my Chinese friends complained to me that I should not take the taxi, 'After all your trips to Beijing, don't you know yet that China is a cycle country?', she said, somewhat annoyed. But on the whole if you feel the need to invest in a bicycle trading business then you are certainly thinking of the wrong country.

6

Chinese exports

The following table shows China's exports during 2007, as provided by the Economic Information Agency (www.jdonline.com.hk). All percentage changes are from 2006 and cover accumulated exports.

Commodity	(US$ billions)	percentage change
Mechanical and electric equipment	56.22	27.9
Hi-tech products	27.78	24.8
Auto-data processing equipment	9.88	36.3
Garments & accessories	9.56	22.9
Textiles (Raw materials & finished goods)	4.60	14.5
Rolled steel	3.71	88.9
Hand-held or wireless Telephone	2.80	14.20
Footwear	2.10	16.1
Furniture	1.76	27.2
Plastic products	1.20	9.2
Toys	0.70	20.1
Aquatic products	0.38	-0.6

Foreign investment

China has always been a attractive market for foreign investment, however, it's only really since the market reforms of the early 1980s and the country's admission to the WTO that corridors have sprung open for foreign investment.

The main benefits for any foreign company, manufacturing or otherwise, establishing a presence in China or a relationship with Chinese companies can be summed up as follows:

- Lower Production costs
- Increased margins and Rates of redemption
- Greater volume of activity
- Access to the Chinese market
- Being close to other emerging markets
  (i.e. India, Japan and Singapore)

In recent years a number of leading international banks and insurance companies have set up JVs with mainland partners, and are able to offer insurance and banking services to native Chinese customers. Having already established a string presence in China, these financial institutions were at last able to benefit from China's new foreign investment regime that resulted from its accord with the WTO in December 2001.

Another advantage that benefits FDIs is the opening up of previously closed or highly restricted business sectors including:

- Banking
- Securities
- Telecommunications
- Trading
- Distribution
- Tourism
- Advertising
- Real Estate
- Management Consulting
- Oil and Gas

For some strategic sectors, the old arrangement of majority Chinese ownership remains in place. As mentioned earlier, it is best to get as much background information on location, market, type of business,

6

International banks

business structure and all other important questions or issues which you may have.

Chapters two and five provide most of the useful information on whom to consult. China may not necessarily have the cheapest manufacturing unit costs in Asia (including the whole of the Far East and Subcontinent), but nevertheless, it is capable of producing volume at what is usually put forward as a 'cost effective' price.

Without a doubt the quality of manufactured goods has improved greatly in recent years, thanks to the great efforts of the Chinese government who are clamping down hard on abusers of the corporate sector. Infrastructure is rapidly improving, and is now capable of coping with the detailed demands of foreign companies investing in China.

6

Finally, for any foreign investor it is always good to know that the country in which they want to set up business in, or engage in business activities with, has a stable and strong government, and that there are no signs of any major depression in the economy due to unforeseen circumstances such as wars or natural disasters. China certainly is a stable place to do business and many think-tanks believe that it is likely to remain a politically stable country for a long time as no country can afford not to make friends with China!

This chapter focuses in detail on some of the major industries that have made a strong impact on the Chinese economy in recent years.

Olympic Games 2008

In the run up to the Olympics in 2008, China invested over US$25billion in building infrastructure in the host cities for the various games, the sports venues themselves, roads, advertising and promotion for the games. When China won the bid way back in 1992, It saw it as an opportunity to really prove itself by making sure that these games would be better than all the others in the history of the tournament. In Chinese culture there is a well known saying: 'If there

6

is an opportunity, then take it...don't waste it', and the Chinese government and people have taken this wonderful opportunity.

There was great interest from foreign companies that invested heavily in Sponsorship and advertising for the different venues. Shanghai General Motors signed a five year sponsorship deal back in 2002, along with twenty other sponsors who forked out over US$3 billion between them. Much of this budget has been allocated towards Beijing's transportation infrastructure, including: expanding the capital's airport with two new runways and a new terminal building that became fully operational in the summer of 2008, expanding the metro system to include three extra lines that were opened in the first half of 2008 as well as tripling the amount of roads (including the new five ring road system around Beijing).

The government also allocated a budget of around US$400 million for upgrading the communications and technology infrastructure to cater for the mass media around the event.

Aerospace

If you go to any of the 400 odd airports in China I guarantee that you will see more people, even at the less popular airports, than you would see at an international airport for a small country such as Luxembourg! China's aviation industry is booming and you would be amazed at the amount of planes Chinese airlines have. Almost every province has their own airline, either run privately or by the government, and this is only the beginning. With over 460 airports and over eighty airlines, China is set to dominate the aviation industry in the next five to ten years, and is likely to overtake some of America's biggest airports and airlines in terms of profits and structural size.

The demand is so high for this industry that Chinese people will soon be flying in planes made in their homeland by Chinese companies, and not by Boeing or Airbus. Aviation experts around the world strongly believe that this could be the start of a trend that will see

China eventually building its own version of the 'Super-Jumbo' (the Airbus A380) in the near future. Indeed, in 2006, the Chinese government confirmed that they are interested in looking into the prospects of having a Chinese made Super Jumbo by the year 2020. It wouldn't be surprising to see this turned into a reality, especially in a country that sent a man into space without any assistance of western organizations.

China Aviation Industry Corporation I (AVIC I, www.avic1.com.cn), a state-run conglomerate based in Shanghai that started building the country's first independently developed regional passenger plane in 2006. The plane has been primarily built for the Chinese market, although the company has plans to start selling the plane to African, South American and Asian countries at a fraction of what it would cost them to buy from Boeing, Airbus or any other western manufacturer. In 2006, Shanghai Airlines placed an order for over 70 ARJ21s planes, due to be delivered in early 2009. Outside the USA, to date China is the biggest market for both Airbus and Boeing, with combined number of aircraft in China from both manufacturers reaching 1100 by the first half of 2008, that's just over ten per cent of the world's planes in China! Boeing has forecasted that by 2025, 28,600 new aircraft will be required worldwide, 3,400 will be required just for the Chinese market!

Agriculture

Of central importance to the Chinese people, agriculture has dominated the Chinese government's agenda time and time again. Farmers' salaries have steadily increased, although not as much as in other professions and industries. China feeds almost a quarter of the world's population and, by 2008, over a third of imported food into the African and South American continents was from China. The main agricultural products in China are rice, wheat, soya, poultry and pork.

As of 2007 figures, China grows two crops of rice each year and produces about 200 million tonnes annually, of which, more than 15 per cent is exported overseas. Traditional buyers of Chinese rice are North Korea, Cuba, Russia and various countries on the African continent.

Rice production

137

6

The automotive industry

Next time you go to China, don't be surprised to see a Ferrari, Mercedes Benz, Jaguar or even an imported Rolls-Royce parked outside, say, a local seafood restaurant! It has become a competitive market and a lucrative business for foreign investors, with Japanese (Honda, Nissan, Toyota), German (Daimler Chrysler), American (Shanghai GM-Wuling) and British (Range Rover, Jaguar) companies either setting up manufacturing facilities in China or forging partnerships with local Chinese who manufacture under license. Increasingly there is a whole new range of Chinese automobile companies which western corporations have probably never even heard of, that are pushing into this market, such as the Cherry QQ in Anhui province.

In the past ten years, China's road network has doubled to over 1.7 million kilometers. The current boom in private car ownership is only the beginning. As incomes grow and bank finance catches on, China is set for an outburst in auto ownership that will dwarf anything the global industry has ever seen. In the third quarter of 2008, there were an estimated eight million automobiles in Beijing, with about a third of these being privately owned.

Education

With its rising economy, there is a great need for foreign teachers in Chinese schools, as more Chinese students than ever before are keen to learn the English language. As in other parts of Asia, in mainland China, American English seems to be more popular than British English and most of the language books are oriented towards American English. Having said that, the British English teaching organisation, English First, which opened its first China office in 1992, now has over ninety learning centres on the mainland. EF was also chosen as one of the official sponsors of the Olympics.

More Chinese students than ever before are graduating with at least a Bachelors degree – by 2008 there were just over five million students gradating from Chinese universities. One student I met at Guangzhou's Guangdong University of Technology in 2005 told me,

'MBAs are being treated like normal diplomas because every student wants to get one in China these days'. The government has made great efforts towards making primary and secondary education compulsory for all children. Another student I met in Shenzhen last year told me that, 'There will be at least twenty graduates in the pipeline for each job vacancy and the competition is so fierce that even a single percentage difference in the final exam result can decide who gets the job.'

Many foreign universities have set up partnerships with Chinese universities. Examples include the recent partnerships between Babson College in Wellesley (USA) and Zhejiang Univerity; and a US$39 campus built by Nottingham University of the UK, in the city of Ningbo (Zhejiang Province) in collaboration with Zhejiang Wanli University was opened in 2005. There are growing numbers of partnerships between Chinese and British universities, although generally speaking they lag behind American, Australian and Canadian educational establishments that have set up Chinese partnerships.

While foreign investors are bringing in revenue to the Chinese economy with their businesses, some foreign educational institutions are taking advantage of the lucrative international education market, by offering expatriate children the chance to get the same education in China that they would receive back home.

Dulwich College Management (DCM) is one of the leading organizations that provides consultation on the establishment of international education in China. DCM has their head office in Shanghai and has in recent years helped the growth of branch schools of famous British public schools on the Chinese mainland. One such example is Dulwich College, which has its roots in south-east London, and by the end of 2007 had three established schools on mainland China accommodating a total of approximately 1200 students between them.

Dulwich College Management
901 Aviation Centre
1600 Nanjing Xi Lu,
Jing'an District
Shanghai 200040 China

Tel: +86 (0)21 6248 7878
Fax: +86 (0)21 6248 6899
Website: www.dulwich-management.com
E-mail: info@dulwich-management.com

Fashion

In a country where prior to 1979, almost everyone used to wear traditional navy blue 'Mao' suits (as worn by Chairman Mao), western fashion is still very much a new concept in China. As well as hosting two annual fashion shows, one in Dalian and the other in the capital city, China has held 'experimental' fashion shows in Shanghai and Guangzhou on smaller scale which have in recent years been successful.

Fashion is more appealing to young middle class Chinese than to the elderly. You will occasionally see older people still wearing their Mao caps and jackets in parts of China. Nevertheless, fashion trends are definitely changing in China; in the major cities, shopping malls are opening more and more western designer stores. GAP, FCUK and Aquascutum all have a major presence in China. Other well known Italian, French and American labels have achieved significant profits from business in China.

Now it is not uncommon to see Nike, Adidas, Caterpillar or DKNY stores in the major cities. In 2007 Burberry had 24 stores on the mainland and two in Hong Kong. In Hong Kong the general culture is more international than on the mainland, and so more people are aware of the latest trends in the west. In Hong Kong, when a new fashion or gadget comes out, people will jump at the first opportunity to buy it. All major international fashion brands have branches in Hong Kong.

The need for good publicity, advertising and promotion is essential in any business but especially in the fashion industry. International magazines, including *Good Housekeeping* and *Men's Health*, are available on the mainland but only in Mandarin. There are also many locally published glossy magazines available.

Food & beverage

Western fast-food restaurants in China were non-existent in the early 1980s and most of them only started operations on the mainland as an experiment in 1987. People used to eat instant noodles or healthy boiled dumplings with rice and some cooked meat (usually roasted). Since the late 1990s there has been a surge of global fast-food chains in China such as MacDonald's, Subway, KFC and Pizza Hut (The latter two both owned by Tricon Global Restaurants Inc). In 2008 there were 1,800 registered KFC stores in over 400 cities across the country; and over 750 MacDonald's in China, which had it first outlet in Beijing in 1995. China's first drive-thru opened in Dongguan city (Guangdong) in the second part of 2005, and the there are plans to establish more in the coming years.

Increasingly global food and shopping chains are establishing their presence in China. In recent years, global household names such as Walmart (USA), Carrefour (France), Papa John's Pizza (USA), Tesco (UK), Starbucks (USA) and Illy Café have firmly established themselves, with numerous stores in all the major cities in China – and are continuing to expand into the more rural areas.

China Beverage Industry Association
www.chinabeverage.org

China Chain Store & Franchise Association
www.ccfa.org.cn

Medical & health care

During the early part of this century, China has successfully fought off a period of uncertainty caused by the SARS and Bird Flu scares. The government put in place strict laws on the checking of poultry and other meat products to be consumed in China or exported, primarily to Hong Kong or Macau.

By the end of 2007, there were an estimated two million cases of HIV in China. China has been actively tackling this problem for many years, setting up government sponsored free health clinics for people in rural areas

6

6

as well as promoting the use of contraception. All foreigners are required to have an HIV blood test before applying for a work visa in China.

WHO The Chinese government is working with the World Health Organization (www.who.org) to assist with all R&D activities by multinationals like Pfizer, GSK etc. to control infectious and endemic diseases.

Healthcare in China is managed by four separate ministry level organizations:

- The Ministry of Health – responsible for the management of healthcare institutions and training of personnel.
- The State Drug Administration (SDA) – regulates the use and production of medical devices and pharmaceutical products.
- The State Administration for Traditional Chinese Medicines.
- The Ministry of Labour and Social Security – responsible for welfare and the establishment of a medical insurance system.

For Pharmaceutical industry, the government has the website:

China Association for Medical Devices Industry
www.camdi.org

Oil & Gas

With over 1.3 billion people, China is the world's second largest oil consumer, behind America. With real GDP steadily increasing at double figures for the past six years, China's requirements for energy are expected to rise by over 140 per cent by 2020. In order to keep abreast of this immense growth, China requires increasing amounts of oil. Good news if you don't like bicycles. Of course, everyone wants planes, cars and trains, but China's thirst for success and modernization is certainly striking alarm bells in stock markets around the world. It is rather frightening to read that China's oil consumption grows by approximately 7.5 per cent per year, seven times faster than America's.

Consequently, by the year 2020, China is expected to have at least eighty times more cars than in 2006. Another reason for the rapid increase in the number of planes, trains and cars is the low price of oil in China. China currently imports about one third of its oil and is expected to double its need for imported oil between 2008 and 2020. In 2007, over half of China's oil imports came from the Middle East and Africa, countries including, Iran, Kuwait, Kazakhstan, Sudan, and Azerbaijan. By 2015, China's share of oil from the Middle East will stand at 70 per cent.

6

China has its own rich reserves of Oil and natural Gas. In the East China Sea, where rich oil and gas reserves are believed to exist, in 2005 China began the exploration process for gas reserves on its side of the East China Sea. **China National Petroleum** (www.cnpc.com.cn) invested over US$800 million in the Sino-Russian pipeline running to the city of Daqing in north-east China. In Southern and Central America, during a visit by top Chinese officials in 2006 (and also the early part of 2007), China concluded lucrative oil and gas deals with Brazil, Peru, Ecuador and Venezuela. Prior to this, a series of oil agreements, signed in early 2005, allowed Chinese companies like China National petroleum and the state owned **China National Offshore Oil Company** (CNOOC, www.cnooc.com.cn) to explore for oil and gas and set up refineries in Venezuela.

Property market

A phenomenal increase in international trade has produced a demand for property that had, until recently, been unheard of. As well as the SAR regions of Hong Kong and Macau, China's large cities, such as Shanghai, Beijing, Shenzhen and Guangzhou have witnessed an increase in house prices to the point where many local people would now be unable to buy the homes in which they live. There is a further element to the Chinese property market, seldom mentioned in the Western media, which is that all the land in China is state owned. There is no existing law in mainland China permitting the acquisition of private land ownership.

All property in China is under a 'land use right' system. There are three types of lease on land: **residential**, which is run on a 70-year lease; **commercial**, which is on a 50-year lease; and **industrial**, on a 40-year lease. The four cities mentioned above are becoming hotspots in the property market for foreign and local investors. Beijing certainly attracted a lot of attention from property developers during the Olympics and is likely to continue to do so for quite some time in the wake of the tournament.

You only have to cross the border from Hong Kong to places like Panyu, near Guangzhou, where state owned companies such as the Zhujiang Real Estate Developers are constructing small towns on the outskirts of the city, like 'Roman Villa', where the architecture of the neighborhood is meant to create the illusion of living in ancient Rome; or 'Mexican Villa', complete with cactuses, sand, yellow painted homes and the feeling that you are in Mexico! Most of these 'Villas' have their own schools, free transportation to the city centre, lakes, golf courses, sports centres and even their own set of convenience stores. Prices are, of course, cheap compared to Europe or America and vary according to the area. In Guangzhou, for a 4 bedroom house with garden in the Roman Villa, a typical price could be around RMB 800,000 (Approx US$ 100,000). It can be a good investment in places such as Beijing or Shanghai considering the amount of attention these places will get around the end of the current decade.

When one reflects on the sheer magnitude of the real estate industry in places like Guangzhou or Beijing, a common question that comes to mind is 'where does all this money come from?' I have been told by many local Chinese people that 5 per cent are developers from Hong Kong or Taiwan, while the other 95 per cent are communist party friendly ex-government officials, who after the market reforms opened in 1979, invested money (usually on loan from the central government) to purchase disused farm land and then repay the loan over time as apartments are sold at a dizzying pace. For the vast majority who did borrow in the 1980s, most have likely already paid back their loans. Although this is the case in all of Chinese industry – it is more apparent in the property market because it is easy to observe the enormous growth at first hand.

Taking this into account it is easy to explain how, in recent years, high numbers of Chinese students have started attending British public schools (remember fees at such schools can be in the region of $40,000 per annum!) or driving the latest Mercedes Benz while still in their first year at an Ivy League college! One friend of mine is already developing a strategic plan of how to manage his father's business in Shanghai – before he has even completed his studies in the US!

Science & Technology

The government has set up three priority areas for development:

- High technology focusing on IT, Semiconductors, biology, new materials, aerospace and manufacturing. All of this is intended to propel China's manufacturing industry into the 21st century.
- Upgrading the technological levels of traditional industries, i.e. making them more efficient and profit driven.
- Having a new science and technology system that is compatible with the requirements of a market economy.

China Ministry of Science & Technology
www.most.gov.cn
Some useful Chinese websites (in English and Chinese) for certain technological sectors are included here:

Engineering and Mechanical products
China Association of Lighting Industry
www.chineselighting.org

China Building Material Industry Association
www.cbminfo.com

China Iron & Steel Association
www.chinaisa.org.cn

China Mining Association
www.chinamining.com.cn

China Construction Machinery Association
www.cncma.org

China Plastics Processing Industry Association
www.cppia.com.cn

Semiconductors and software
China Software Industry Association
www.csia.org.cn

Internet Society of China
www.isc.org.cn

China Association for Science and Technology
www.cast.org.cn

Telecommunications

Two major Chinese companies are dominating the global Telecoms market. Huawei Technologies (www.huawei.com) and ZTE Corporation (www.zte.com), both have their headquarters in Shenzhen, and both were started in the late 1980s by Chinese entrepreneurs who saw the opportunity of growth provided by the Special Economic Zone in Guangdong province. Both of these companies specialise in the manufacturing of mobile and fixed telecommunications equipment for service providers around the world. In 2007, Huawei technologies reached a turnover of over US$12 billion and is considered China's number one company to work for.

In the country, China Telecom and China Netcom are the fixed-line businesses, China Mobile and China Unicom are in the mobile sector, as well as two smaller companies: China Satcom and China TieTong. As of July 2008, China had over 610 million fixed-line subscribers and approximately 560 million mobile customers. Other than that all major international telecom manufacturing companies including Siemens, Cisco, and Nortel Networks have a presence in China.

China Information Industry
www.cnii.com.cn/ecnii/

Tourism

China's tourism industry is one of the fastest-growing industries in the national economy and is also one of the industries with a very distinct global competitive edge. The total revenue of China's tourism industry reached US$ 83.2 billion in 2008. Tourism has become the main source of tax revenue and the key industry for economic development in the provinces of Guangxi, Guangdong, Beijing, Jiangsu and Sichuan. Other areas where the majority of income has been from tourism include Tibet and the Xinjiang autonomous regions.

The total number of tourists to China was just over 118 million in 2008. This was set to increase even after the Olympics finished as people flock to see the sites and sounds of China that they saw on television during the tournament.

China's domestic tourism market makes up over 90 per cent of the country's tourism traffic, and contributes in excess of 70 per cent of total tourism revenue. A large middle class population with strong consumption power is emerging in China, especially in major cities. Currently there are 65 countries/areas open to Chinese tour groups and so in 2008, over 22 million Chinese went overseas for holiday tours. The World Tourism Organization (WTO) forecasted that China's tourism industry will take up to 8.6 per cent of world market share to become the world's top tourism industry by 2020.

China National Tourism Administration
www.cnta.gov.cn

Other industries:
Construction industry

The growth in the economy has been fuelled by the large amounts of road infrastructure, hospitals, schools, Olympic stadiums, airports, and the numerous real estate projects that are growing out of reclaimable land in the major cities around the country. A major market for good quality decorating materials, in the latest fashion, colors and styles etc. is also being driven by the demands of Chinese consumers who pay attention to the smallest detail. It is a recognised fact that, in China, the use of

6

building materials continues to grow at a faster rate than the overall economic growth of the country.

The key domestic competitors in the Chinese construction industry are:

- China State Construction Engineering Corporation (www.cscec.com)
- Shanghai Construction Group (www.scacgroup.com)
- Beijing Construction Engineering Group Co., Ltd. (www.dsaaa.com)
- Beijing Urban Construction Group Co., Ltd (www.bucg-intl.com)

Do-It-Yourself (DIY)

The British company, B&Q opened its first China store in 1999. Now it operates 64 outlets across the country (including the world's biggest B&Q store in Beijing) and is aiming to increase the number of stores by 8 to 12 per year as the explosion in housing construction increases demand for home furnishings. B&Q China, which sells products ranging from sofas to vacuum cleaners, opened 10 new stores in 2007, increasing overall sales by 41 per cent and exceeding by far the $55 billion market's 15 to 20 per cent growth.

The Swedish DIY giant, IKEA opened their first store in Shanghai in 2003 and by July of 2008, the organization had six stores on the mainland in all the major cities (including Nanjing and Shenzhen). The home furnishing firm spent over US$80m on a distribution centre in Shanghai as well as new stores in Chengdu, Guangzhou and Beijing.

Soap and Detergent Industry

China Association of Surfactant Soap and Detergent Industry (CASSDI)
www.cassdi.org

Textiles

The majority of the textile industry is either based in the Pearl River Delta in Guangdong Province or around the Shangahi/Suzhou area in Jiangsu province. The latter is famous for producing Chinese silk products while the former is popular for all types of exported textile. In 2007 the total amount of textile imports into China were around US$3.9 million, while exports were approximately US$46 million in the same year.

China National Garment Association
www.cnga.org.cn

China Feather & Down Industrial Association
www.cfd.com.cn

Toys Industry
China Toy Association
www.toy-cta.org

6

Loyalty schemes

China is the world's largest consumer market, and it also happens to be a culture strongly driven by a loyalty concept; by this I mean you will see a lot of: 'buy this, get that free' on almost every service or product you come across. Even with a bottle of water in a local 'Seven-Eleven' store, you may get a pack of free chocolates etc. The Chinese loyalty scheme market is set to grow faster than anything the world has seen before because, unlike other countries where it is just a means to grow your business, in China it is also part of the culture to offer something extra with a product as a kind of gift. There are many examples of Loyalty schemes in China, some more recent ones are:

1. Every month MacDonald's, Pizza Hut and KFC offer 'coupons' to consumers to encourage them to buy the latest fast-food product. E.g. buy one meal, get second free etc.
2. Entrance tickets to beauty salons or foot massage – buy ten tickets for the price of seven etc.
3. Even in some hotels, if you stay for a certain period you may get something extra like free gym or dinner ticket etc.
4. Air China, Shenzhen Airlines and many other airlines in China offer tempting loyalty schemes to lure passengers on to flights.

7

establishing a presence in China

7

establishing a presence in China

The aim of this section is to provide a sweeping overview for the visitor who is considering the possibility of a local office. Here are some of the pitfalls and benefits, an insight into the legal situation, and some of the major issues to be considered, such as recruiting, finding premises, etc.

How to set up a permanent operation

This chapter sets out to clarify the main points and provide a general overview of how to go about setting up a permanent business operation in China.

China is a country that is going through rapid change almost every day, and it is not like London or Paris where things will remain the same for months, so it is difficult to provide an accurate picture. However, what this chapter will do is provide information about the main factors which you should consider as a key decision maker in your organisation: location, timing, choosing partners etc. There is solid proof that others have succeeded, as of 2007 there were over 2,160 multinational companies in China and 1,620 multinational companies in Hong Kong.

7

Try out the market

Before even considering exploring the prospect of setting up a business in China, if you have the chance then it may be worthwhile to go to one of the major cities either with a trade mission or as a tourist just to get a taste of what the place is like. It will be a shock for someone who has not been to China before – but also exciting, which adds to the glamour of international business and travel to and from Asia.

A long haul

Factors to consider when making the decision to set up a business interest in China:

- **Effort** – As an international business leader you will no doubt need to visit your office in China or attend important meetings with clients, suppliers and potential partners on location rather than using digital methods (Video conference etc). Long haul traveling can be fun for the first two trips, but after a while it becomes tedious and stressful; especially if you have a family and you have to be away for long periods at a time.

- **Time** – setting up a business is not something that happens overnight; there will be many obstacles along the way.

- **Determination** – Once you have started, there is no going back and things can only get better if you are strongly focused on your goals.
- **Financial Capacity** – In China it is important that targets are met without you or your client or Partner being in a situation where either party loses face because financial requirements have not been met. This is more important once a MOU (Memorandum of Understanding) is signed.
- **Success** – This brings in all the above points together. This requires constant watch over the whole business so that you, financiers and shareholders have no reservations. Taking chances and keeping pressure over business interests is all part of the game. There is a Chinese saying 'He who doesn't throw the dice can never expect to score a six!'

General guidelines

Before embarking to set up a joint venture:

- Carry out plenty of research on the destination and establish that a market exists for your particular business.
- Target the opportunities, meet potential clients and make your decision on the sales strategy you are planning to use.
- Focus on what you want to achieve and avoid doing deals un-registered business owners or being led into a fantasy by scams that offer multi-million dollar payouts.
- Be aware of companies that pretend to be consultants or foreign collection agencies, but are, in actual fact, not professional in their approach and have an endless list of company logos on their letterheads or literature. These are another set of professional 'scammers' who are only interested in your wallet.
- Are the firms you are talking to agents, distributors or end users? Understanding the characteristics of different markets is vital to your business's growth; dealing with middle men can sometimes be a problem, so you need to decide if you really want to do it. Some companies prefer

their clients to be end-users or OEMs (Original Equipment Manufacturers).

After securing your business partner or client in China, signing your first deal can be the means to securing more business, and the beginning of your entry into a market that could change the fortunes of your company.

If, however, months, or even years (it can take that long in China!), pass without securing an order, it is time to question your sales philosophy and approach to the market. Was it the wrong market for you? Did you choose the wrong location? Could you have approached the deal differently by using better trained/experienced sales people? Was it a problem of people management due to cultural differences? Or was it just not the right product for the market?

If you feel that your local contact, or their lack of enthusiasm, may be the reason why you have had a poor start on the market in China, then you will have lost only time, and not a great deal of money. You will also have gained some valuable experience along the way.

Legal disputes

Another major problem that you may encounter in China is that clients may change their minds even after the contract has been signed. In my time in China I have had the 'pleasure' of coming across such cases more often than I would like! For example, if the Terms & Conditions (T&Cs) state that the Chinese client or partner needs to pay 'x' per cent of the total amount due upfront before the delivery of the products, but the client decides not to go ahead with the deal after signing the contract. The client might believe that they should not pay anything because either they have lost the contract, or the person who signed the contract isn't employed by their company anymore. Inevitably these sorts of situations lead to a legal case – and in China such legal disputes can take years without being resolved – sometimes costing more money in legal fees than the original deal itself!

Local conformity

Your products must be able to conform to local regulations, of which there are too many! Each province in China has its own test authority and many products need to be tested independently before they can enter the market place. Acceptance of your product in one province may not necessarily mean that it will be accepted in another province. It is best to ask the local government office in your province or consult your consulate, or if you are lucky you may be able to get some sound advice and assistance from a local businessman – this where your networking skill or 'Guangxi' comes into effect.

7

Establishing a representative office

Once you have secured orders and are comfortable with you local arrangement, then it is time to think seriously about setting up a representative office on the mainland. As mentioned before, there are a whole host of organizations that can offer advice, most of them are listed in chapters 2, 5 and 6. The best approach is to get in touch with your Chamber of Commerce first and then carry out fundamental research using management consultancies and other channels.

You need to make sure that you choose well educated local management staff members who you know can manage the local office and be trustworthy in your absence. Normally multinationals tend to recruit anyone who has at least degree level education and speaks good English; whereas smaller foreign startups unfamiliar with China cannot afford to take such risks and tend to employ experienced, western educated native Chinese managers, who understand the western cultural mindset, both the business and personal aspects (such as people management), as well as having a detailed local knowledge of the domestic market in which they are located. Setting up a business in Shanghai is not exactly the same as setting up a business in say, Guangzhou for example, because there are cultural differences in the way people in different provinces think.

With your representative office, you can exercise greater control of your China operations and respond rapidly to market conditions.

Expansion

When you have established your representative office, the next step is to plan a strategy allowing you to expand to other locations. The main challenge any foreign or domestic business will face in China is that it is not a single market but rather a cluster of markets. Every province is like a small country within a large country, because every province has its own localized legislation, laws, smaller government and airline.

Appointing distributors, sales agents and so on in different provinces and increasing your outlets throughout China as part of a planned programme will be of vital importance to the development of your business. Always be on the lookout for competition in China.

In the medium term, there are several options available to you. It may be worthwhile considering establishing a Wholly Owned Foreign Enterprise (WOFE) as a representative on the mainland. In that way you are able to control the major day to day running of the company while the local representative office can act as a China Holding Company. There is no point in making arrangements for expansion in the export markets if it is going to impact upon your domestic situation. This set up may not provide the security of a formal Chinese Holding Company (CHC), but may be better suited for a Small to Medium Sized Enterprise (SME). In the process, on long term prospects, it would be beneficial for you to set up a firm manufacturing base alongside the representative office. Another option is to work alongside an existing Foreign Investment Enterprise (FIE) that is already established within your specialized industry, and has a well cemented country-wide sales and distribution network. Most importantly working alongside them may reduce your overheads.

7

By working closely with other foreign investors and local business professionals as well as getting some sound advice from your Chamber of Commerce etc., you will be in a better position to manage your business and be able to overcome any challenges which you are likely to meet when setting up a representative office in China.

Guidelines for expansion

Investigate thoroughly who your competitors are in the market and the area in which you are locating your business. Investing in China for the long term needs solid commitment and if you are a small business then that commitment may require you to relocate to China in order to manage the people and functions of the business better – because no one apart from yourself would know what's best for your business. Any new foreign company in China, especially a SME needs to be looked after constantly, just like a baby, otherwise it is easy to lose track of business activities and important issues that may require your attention.

Also consider other factors, such as any impact of, say, closing down one of your offices or manufacturing facilities in favor of another location – would that be a good move for you? Will you really need to close down that office to offset other opportunities in China? Take you time, win orders and get yourself established as a brand or a name on the market before making any move towards investment.

If you enter into a JV agreement then it would be wise to keep your manufacturing process and facilities separate from the sales and distribution set up. There are not many Chinese manufacturers with effective combined sales and distribution arrangements. Examples of these that come to mind include Mengniu, China's leading dairy products company (www.mengniu.com.cn) among others. The cultures of manufacturing and sales should be kept apart and also financed separately.

Because China is such a large and complex market, any foreign business should plan, in the medium to long term, for regional manufacturing facilities, not necessarily with the same partner, while managing control of the sales and distribution network.

You could perhaps consider an assembly operation in the WOFE form, which would give you legal and direct control over your sales and distribution. Also be aware that the import and export laws of China are different from other markets, and tax laws are strict – the tax can be as high as 70 per cent on some traded goods. Be sure to check carefully and investigate all the resources provided in this book.

Location

7

- Because of the size and complexity of China, it's usually not a good option to invest in multiple locations all at once.
- Check with your local Trade & Investment office or your Chamber of Commerce for some sound advice on location if you are unsure.
- Think about the logistics of distribution – accessibility to airports, seaports, major roads etc. are all important considerations.
- Look carefully at the prospects for exporting from China as there are tax incentives for bringing foreign currency into the country and exports are a major source of income.
- It is a good idea to have a business deal with a Hong Kong based company because by working together they can assist you to set up operations in Guangzhou, Shenzhen or the 'industrial beehive' of Dongguan.
- Deciding between Hong Kong and the mainland can be a tricky task. If you are thinking of starting out in Hong Kong and then making inroads to the mainland, then bear in mind that in Hong Kong over 92 per cent of the population speak Cantonese, whereas Mandarin is the main language in China – so it may be that you will first set foot into Guangdong province (if coming from Hong Kong).

Distribution

All the deals have been signed, the location is chosen and your manufacturing plant is set. Now the most important decision to make is choosing the type of distribution method to get your goods to the client or between company offices in an international space in a safe, secure and quick way.

Generally speaking, the quality of warehousing facilities in China is not as good as in Europe or North America because warehouse mechanical equipment is not as modern as one would want. On a positive note, delays are not as severe as they used to be because of better logistics system; better management and training is provided to the workers, and some workers can speak and read conversational English too, which can be reassuring to companies if the address on the cargo is only written in English.

There are a growing number of FIEs who have seen the gap in the market and are able to provide secure and reliable warehousing services together with a distribution network.

All channels of transport are used by companies. Sea, Air and land freight are all efficient when trading goods between China and overseas. The Chinese government has been investing a lot of budget for the past few years in improving road infrastructure, building new airports and improving the major sea ports.

Air freight is expensive, however if you are after speed and peace of mind that your goods will be delivered at the destination in a secure way, then this may be the best option. Sea freight is usually used for bulk containers that contain large sized goods, but of course can take weeks or months to get to your destination, and there is a chance that not all goods will be delivered because goods can get lost in the system. Rail, which is state owned in China, can also take days if sending goods from, say Beijing to Guangzhou and is not that reliable or secure.

Communications

China is one of the world's fastest growing markets for telephones and internet applications. In 2008, there were over 450 million fixed-line subscribers and over 570 million mobile customers – that's more than one and half times the population of the USA. In 2008, more than one out of three had a fixed telephone subscription and more than 1.48 million mobile phone subscribers sign up in China every week. For Hong Kong, in 2007, there were over 3.8 million exchange lines. The telephone density was 95 lines per 100 households or over 55 per cent by population, which is among the highest in the world.

7

Beijing

Detailed street maps are available in all major hotels

Beijing

Beijing

The nation's capital

The capital city of the People's Republic of China, Beijing, like many capital cities around the world, is not truly symbolic of the country it represents. There will always be a strong Chinese feel and influence to the city, but, since the early 1980s, it has become more multicultural. Beijing is similar to London or New York in that it has many diverse cultures that are not necessarily representative of the country as a whole. The major cities of most countries are too cosmopolitan in their character to show what life is really like outside the constraints and influences of big city life.

Geography

The city, with a population of over thirteen million people, lies in northern China surrounded by the provinces of Hebei and Tianjin. The most striking thing any first time visitor notices about Beijing is how symmetrical the city is; laid out in an East-West and North-South design. It is one of the worlds most carefully planned and laid out cities. Parks, roads and buildings are laid out as mirror images on either side. Unlike other cities in China, Beijing is becoming modern at a dizzying pace while keeping its ancient historical features intact – there are areas of Beijing where people still live as they would have done hundreds if not thousands of years ago. Then there are the historic buildings lying side by side with large concrete blocks that have high shining glass, which makes Beijing, look similar to any western metropolis. Traffic on the roads is also becoming a huge problem, with an increasing number of Chinese purchasing private cars; mix all of that with the erratic way of driving (i.e. people not giving way to others). Sometimes in the rush hour, you will find it hard to distinguish whether you are in Beijing or New York!

Beijing's 'Silicon Valley' is located in the north-eastern areas of Shangdi and Qi Er Xi, where the likes of IBM Lenovo, P&G and many others have their China HQ offices. China's most prestigious seats of learning are also located around here, including Beijing and Qinghua universities (around the Wu Dao Kou area). Remarkably a quarter of the city's population is employed in the administrative industry.

8

Climate

Beijing is blessed with all four seasons, just like America and the UK. Winters are freezing with well below zero temperatures, while the summers are very hot and humid. Beijing's climate is defined as one of 'continental monsoon'. The four seasons are distinctly recognizable with a temperate spring, rainy summer, clear autumn, and a cold, snowy winter. The best time to be in Beijing is during the spring and autumn, especially during the months of April, May, September and October. It is generally considered that autumn is the best time to visit Beijing because the skies are clear and the weather is comfortable. The average temperature throughout the year is approximately fifteen degrees Celsius. The coldest month is January with an average temperature of approximately minus five degrees Celsius and the hottest month is July at an average temperature of approx twenty eight degrees Celsius. Unfortunately, spring and autumn are shorter than summer and winter. There are occasional sand storms that drift in from the Gobi Desert and the Inner Mongolia region. I remember waking up one morning in September 2005, and the view from my hotel window was something I had never seen before – everything (roads, cars, buildings etc.) was covered in sand – it was a bit like seeing yellow coloured snow. The only difference is that the snow melts away whereas sand needs to be cleaned away afterwards, which can be a tough job for the authorities.

Getting around
Buses

Beijing has a numbered system by which you can distinguish the type of bus operating. Buses that are numbered in the 200s are used for night service. Buses that are numbered in the 800s are air conditioned and comfortable to travel in, while the rest of Beijing's buses are older, more crowded and shabbier than public transport in other cities. It is not uncommon to see a bus jam packed even at 6 am on a Sunday morning. There are four major bus stations in Beijing.

1. **Deshengmen bus Station** is located within walking distance of both Gulou and Jishuitan subway stations. Deshengmen serves routes to the

8

north of the capital, including (at the time
of writing) an express service running every
15 minutes to the Badaling Great wall.

2.   **Dongzhimen bus station** is located close to
the subway station that bears the same name.
It is close to the expat area and Sanlitun, where
most of the embassies are to be found.

3.   **Majuan bus station** is located on Guanqumenwei
Dajie in the south-east of the city and serves most
long distance destinations to the east and south
of the city.

4.   **Yongdongmen bus station** is located in the south
of the city next to the train station that bears the
same name. There are plenty of long distance
buses available to various destinations within
Hebei province and to Tianjin and connections
by rail to other cities in China.

8

Air travel

The capital's only passenger operated airport, Beijing
Capital International Airport, is located approximately
28km to the northeast of the city centre. The airport has
gone through some refurbishment, with new runways
and terminal buildings, all in preparation for the Beijing
2008 summer Olympics when the airport was at its
busiest. Over sixty international and domestic airlines
use the airport. In 2007 Beijing airport handled more
than twenty-seven million passengers.

Taxies

Taxies are ubiquitous, metered and available twenty-four
hours a day. The base rate at the time of writing is ten
Yuan (Approx $1.50) between 06:00AM and 23:00pm
for the first mile. Bear in mind that taxies are not
allowed to drop off or pick up passengers around
the roads surrounding Tiananmen Square.

Metro and trains

In 2007, Beijing had three metro lines (Lines 1, 2
and 5) in operation and an overground train line
(Line thirteen). Line two runs in a circular pattern
around the city. It has connections with line thirteen
at Xizhimen (to the North West of the city) and
Dongzhimen (to the North East of the city). Line one

runs in an East-West direction across the city centre between Pingyuoyuan and Sihui Dong station. The subway operates between 5.30am and 11pm seven days a week. Tickets for using the metro are priced at three Yuan per single journey, irrespective of how many stops you make and can be used if you change lines. If your journey to the city centre starts on line thirteen, then the price is five Yuan per single trip.

Three more metro lines (Line 8, Line 10 and the Airport Line) became fully operational in July of 2008 ahead of the Olympic games. There are plans to expand the subway system to meet the city's growing need. The proposal is to have 19 lines in opperation by 2015; construction on many of these new lines has already begun.

8

Beijing subway system requires you to purchase small paper slips from the ticket office. These need to be shown to a station attendant before you enter the platform.

There are two main stations in Beijing: Beijing Zhan and Beijing Xi Zhan (Beijing West Station). The former is located in the city centre while the latter is located just south of the Junshi Gowuguan subway. Beijing Xi Zhan was opened in 1996. It is more modern and larger in size than Beijing Zhan and caters for destinations to the north and west of the city. Beijing Zhan is used for destinations to the south and east of the city (Shanghai for example).

Food and shopping

Beijing has plenty of restaurants that cater for all kinds of tastes. In 2006 there were over 8,370 restaurants registered in the capital! The most famous dishes are: roasted Duck, Beijing hot pot (boiled meat balls, slices of meat and various vegetables) and dried fruit.

One of the places where most expats tend to flock to for a beer after a long hard week is either to **Charlie's Bar**, which is located in the Jianguo Hotel on Jianguomenwai Dajie, or the **Hard Rock Café** located in the west wing of the Landmark Towers building. There are various other bars where its nice to meet with like minded professionals to cool your heels with a beer after a long day in the office, including the bars inside the **Lido Hotel** (Lido Binguan), which is located on the 4th Ring road, about 5km in the North-east of the city.

The **Friendship store** on Jianguimenwai is a good place to start for shopping, if you want to take back any souvenirs or gifts. It has a large stock of tourist goods such as food, Beijing wine, drinks, toys, Beijing dried fruit and other gifts.

One recommended restaurant in the San Li Tun area that springs to mind is '**Morel's**' (Molaolongxi Xicanting) – a Belgian Restaurant with a well respected Belgian chef and owner whose surname this eatery goes by. Morel's is located opposite the Worker's Gymnasium north gate in the expat area where all the Embassies are based.

The two major areas for shopping are **Xidan** and **Wangfujing**. Xidan is located to the west of Tiananmen Square and Wangfujing to the east. Both have a wealth of shops and restaurants, some offering the usual gifts and name brands, while others offer things out of the ordinary such as cushions that contain self-heating crystals (once a button is pressed a chemical reaction causes the crystals to heat up and turn the hard bag of crystals into a soft hot cushion that can be used to keep warm at night).

China's biggest indoor shopping mall, known as the **Lufthansa Shopping Centre**, is located in Beijing. As well as shops and restaurants, the mall houses corporate and government offices (including airlines) as well as a large multi-story car park.

Beijing's IT Centre (or Computer City as people call it) is located at **Zhongguancun**. Here you can find all of the latest (mostly genuine) cameras and electronic equipment. As always be on the look-out for fake goods and always make sure to ask if the products have a worldwide guarantee supplied in the package.

8

Places of interest

Beijing's rich history and presence as the seat of government and education in China makes it a natural destination that is also full of great tourist attractions.

Tiananmen Square is one of the largest open squares in the world and is said to be able to accommodate up to a million people. The square has borne witness to many important events in China's colourful history. The most infamous of these was the declaration of the founding of the People's Republic of China by Chairman Mao on October 1st 1949. Mao's portrait looms over the square admiring the beautiful views, with the Forbidden City to one side and his mausoleum (where his body lies in state) to the other.

Towards the west of the square is the **People's Hall** (Renmin Da Hiutang) and on the east are the **Museum of Chinese History** and the **Museum of Revolution**. **Mao's Mausoleum** lies in the south of the square where the great man's body lies in state. It is open to public view for a short while everyday.

Towards the north of the Forbidden City is **Beihei Park** (Beihai Gong Yuan), home to the famous wall of nine dragons and the former palace of the Mongol Emperor Kublai Khan. To the south of the Forbidden City is the amazing and unmistakable **Tian Tan** (Temple of Heaven), lies splendidly in the middle of Beihai Park. Inside the park are two beautiful and admirable structures, **Qiniandian** (Hall of Prayer for good Harvests) and **Hianqiutan** (Alter of Heaven).

There are two historical palaces located in the west of the city, **Yi Hi Yuan** (Summer Palace) and **Yuan Ming Yuan**. Yi He Yuan is a large landscaped palace made up of small parks, gardens, romantic pathways and temples. It houses a large lake, called the **Kunming He** which covers approximately twenty-four square kilometres. The landmark of the Summer Palace is the **Pagoda of the Incense of Buddha** (Foxiange) on top of Wanshou Shan, which overlooks Lake Kunming.

Outside the city there are a numerous beautiful parks. In the west of the city there is **Xiang Shan** (Lotus Mountain)

8

and the **Beijing Botanical Gardens**. Both of these attractions can take a whole day to experience in full. The best time to visit Xiang Shan is in the autumn when the leaves are red and the scenery from the peak is breathtaking.

An exciting and adventurous place for both adults and children is the **Beijing Zoo**, located near the Xizhimen station. It is home to many cute young Pandas as well as other exotic animals. The Zoo also has its own restaurant (Binfengtan), which offers many Chinese culinary delights such as fresh pheasant, turtle and deer meat to name just a few!

Accommodation

Here are some renowned hotels where you can stay in Beijing when on business trip. A list of some more good hotels in Beijing is provided in Appendix 1.

Plaza Royale Hotel *****
No.23 West Dawang Road, Chaoyang District
Tel: +86 (0)10 5879 6666;
Website: www.plazaroyale.com.cn

Xinyuan Hotel Beijing *****
No. 6, Shifangyuan, Haidian District
Tel: 86 (0)10 6390 1166;
Website: http://xinyuan.sinotour.com/

The Peninsula Beijing *****
No.8 Goldfish Lane, Wangfujing
Tel: + 86 (0)10 8516 2888;
Website: http://beijing.peninsula.com/

China World Hotel Beijing *****
No. 1 Jianguomenwai Avenue
Tel: + 86 (0)10 6505 2266;
Website: www.shangri-la.com

Novotel Xinqiao Hotel, Beijing ****
No. 2 Dongjiao Min Xiang
Tel: + 86 (0)10 6513 3366;
Website: www.novotel.com

8

Holiday Inn Shangdi ****
No. 33 Shangdi East Road, Haidian District
Tel: + 86 (0)10 82709999;
Website: www.ichotelsgroup.com

TianRui Hotel, Beijing ****
No.15 Bai Shu Hutong, Dong Cheng District
Tel: +86 (0)10 6526 6699;
Website: www.tianrui.com.cn

Marriott Executive Apartments Beijing Palm Springs ***
No. 8 Chaoyang Park South Road, Chaoyang District
Tel: +86 (0)10 6585 5566;
Website: www.marriott.com

International schools in Beijing

Australian International School Beijing
7 Louzizhuang Road
Chaoyang District;
Beijing 100018
Tel.:   +86 (0)10 84394315-6
Fax: +86 (0)10 84391583
E-mail: enquiries@aisb.cn
Website: www.aisb.cn

Beijing City International School
77 Baiziwan Nan Er Road
Beijing 100022, China
Tel: +86 (0)10 8771 7171
Fax: +86 (0)10 8771 7778
E-mail: info@bcis.cn
Website: http://www.bcis.cn

British International School in Beijing
17, Area 4
An Zhen Xi Li
Chaoyang District
Beijing, 100029, China
Tel: +86 (0)10 6443 3151
Fax: +86 (0)10 6443 3156
E-mail: admissions@biss.com.cn
Website: www.biss.com.cn

British School of Beijing
E-mail: info@britishschool.org.cn
Website: www.britishschool.org.cn

Shunyi Campus
Cuizhu Xin Cun, Linyin Road
Tianzhu Town, Shunyi District
Beijing 101312, CHINA
Tel: +86 (0)10 6458 0884
Fax: +86 (0)10 6458 0509

Sanlitun Campus
5 Xiliujie, Sanlitun Road
Chaoyang District
Beijing 100027, CHINA
Tel: +86 (0)10 8532 3088
Fax: +86 (0)10 8532 3089

Dulwich College International Beijing
89 Capital Airport Road
Legend Garden Villas
Shunyi District
Beijing 101300 PRC
Tel: +86 (0)10 6454 9000
Fax: +86 (0)10 6454 9001
E-mail: admissions@dcbeijing.cn
Website: www.dcbeijing.cn

Eton International School
(Not related to the famous Eton College in the U.K)
Palm Springs International Apartments
8 Chaoyang Park South Road
Chaoyang District, Beijing 100026
Tel: +86 (0)10 6539 7171
Fax: +86 (0)10 6539 8817
E-mail: info@etonkids.com
Website: www.etonkids.com

International School of Beijing- Shunyi
10 An Hua Street
Shunyi District
Beijing, 101300, China
Tel: +86 (0)10 8149 2345
Fax: +86 (0)10 8046 2001

8

E-mail: isb-info@isb.bj.edu.cn
Website: www.isb.bj.edu.cn

Harrow School International Beijing
5, 4th Block
Anzhenxili
Chao Yang District
Beijing 100029
Tel: +86 (0)10 6444 8900
Fax: +86 (0)10 6445 3870
E-mail: enquiries@harrowbeijing.cn
Website: www.harrowbeijing.cn

The International Children's House
English Montessori Kindergarten
China World Trade Centre
North Lodge
1 Jian Guo Men Wai Avenue
Beijing 100004
Phone: +86 (0)10 6505-3869, 6505-2288 Ext.81299
Fax: +86 (0)10 6505-1237
E-mail: info@montessoribeijing.com
Website: www.montessoribeijing.com

Western Academy of Beijing
PO Box 8547
10 Lai Guang Ying Dong Lu
Chao Yang District
Beijing, 100103, China
Tel: +86 (0)10 8456 4155
Fax: +86 (0)10 6437 5935
E-mail: hr@westernacademy.com
Website: www.wab.edu

Yew Chung International School
Honglingjin Park, No 5 Houbalizhuang
Chaoyang District
Beijing, 100025, China
Tel: +86 (0)10 8583 3731
Fax: +86 (0)10 8583 2734
E-mail: bisinq@ycef.com
Website: www.ycef.com

Useful Beijing links

www.ebeijing.gov.cn
Official Government website for Beijing

www.thatsbj.com
Monthly expat magazine for Beijing

www.beijingpage.com
Official Directory of all things in Beijing

www.beijingimpression.com
Website for Beijing tours- in and around Beijing

www.bjreview.com.cn
Weekly news- online edition

www.beijingtrip.com
Tour operator- with tours in and around Beijing

www.bjsubway.com
The corporate website of Beijing subway

8

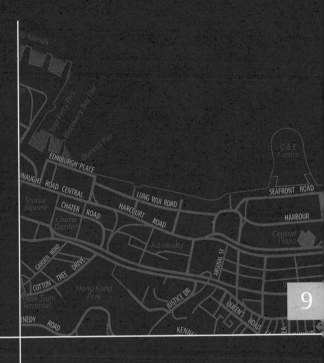

9

other major cities

other major cities

This chapter focuses on some of the other cities in China. The three major cities in China that have a substantial number of expatriates living in them, aside from the capital, are: Shanghai, Guangzhou and Shenzhen. These cities are seen as major international gateways to the outside world. Both Shanghai and Guangzhou have been well established international cities for hundreds of years, while Shenzhen is remarkably less than thirty years old – it used to be an ordinary fishing village on the border of Hong Kong until 1978 when it was classed as one of the five special Economic Zones of China (the other four being Xiamen, Dalian, Hainan Island and Shantou.

Guangzhou

Guangzhou is the capital of Guangdong province and is the industrial hub of southern China. It is sometimes referred to as Canton by westerners. For many travellers Guangzhou is still the first real taste of China once they cross the border from Hong Kong. First impressions of Guangzhou are of a noisy, muggy and polluted city.

Guangzhou is famous for its great food and its biannual trade fair, known as the Canton fair. Among many other trade fairs in China, the Canton fair (which takes place every April and October) is by far the biggest and most popular. It is a huge market where traders from around the world come to Guangzhou to find a good deal for all kinds of 'Made in China' goods.

Established as one of the thirteen new development zones in 1984, Guangzhou has increasingly attracted key industries including; food and beverage (noodle and beer processing are two of the biggest local industries), building materials, electronics, chemicals, machinery, textiles and furniture. Guangzhou also has a high technology zone with the lowest wages and land costs in the Pearl River Delta. Some of the traditional mainstay industries that are present in Guangzhou and the Pearl River Delta are as follows:

9

- Automobile Projects, such as Guangzhou-Honda who have a huge plant just on the outskirts of the city.

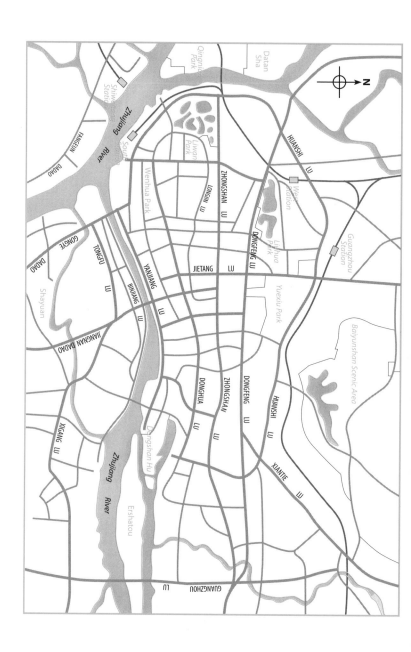

Guangzhou

- Pearl River Steelworks Projects.
- Relocation of Guangzhou Cement factory.
- Guangzhou export processing zone.

Geography

Guangzhou is situated in the Pearl River Delta area and is approximately two hours by train from Hong Kong or about 30 minutes flying time. Some businessmen take the shuttle flights with China Southern Airlines in order to save the hassle of crossing the border at Shenzhen (which can take over 3 to 4 hours at peak hours).

The proximity to Hong Kong has been an important factor in attracting foreign investment into the region. There are more foreign investment corporations in Guangdong province than any other in China. International Hotels, Property investment companies as well as a large number of foreign managed SME businesses have sprung up in the Pearl River Delta in the past ten years, and foreign investment is continuing to rise. Many Chambers of Commerce are investing heavily in attracting foreign businesses to set up their base here.

Both the British and US Consulates-General are located in Guangzhou (and of course other countries Consulates too). Many companies' trade offices are opening in Guangzhou or are being expanded. The city's concentration of businesses and potential trade or investment partners makes Guangzhou the choice for many foreign investors over other cities in China.

Climate

For the majority of the year Guangzhou has a tropical climate with a relative humidity between seventy and ninety per cent, which makes it very sticky and soggy; not ideal if you need to wear an expensive business suit all day! The year is made up of a subtropical-tropical, humid monsoonal climate with a rainy season from April to September and occasional typhoons from May to November. The majority of offices, trade and exhibition halls and homes have air conditioning. When on a formal business visit it is always good to drink lots of fresh water to avoid dehydration, as most of your time

9

will be spent walking or talking. Also be careful when going from one extreme to another. From personal experience I can say that in China most offices are air-conditioned to be far colder than they need to be – it sometimes feels as if it is almost freezing inside. To go from this environment straight to the baking hot outdoors can make you feel ill; it is not good for the body to jump suddenly from one extreme temperature to another.

Transportation

Buses

Guangzhou has two major bus stations, plus a number of smaller lesser used ones scattered around the city. The main bus station is located at Guangzhou Dong Zhan (Guangzhou East Station). You can get buses from here to almost any destination in the city, as well as buses to surrounding towns and villages.

Long distance buses use the provincial bus station which is near the Guangzhou train station on Huanshi Xi Lu. Liuhua bus station, which is close by, also caters for passengers who want long distance journeys.

Air travel

Guangzhou has one major international airport, the Guangzhou Baiyun International airport. This is located about 32km to the north west of the city centre. In 2008, over fifty international, domestic and cargo airlines operated from Baiyun airport and an estimated 25.2 million passengers arrived or departed from here in 2007.

Taxies

Taxies are cheap and can be stopped anywhere at any time. They are metered and are available 24 hours a day.

Trains and Metro

Guangzhou has two main train stations, Guangzhou train station (Guangzhou Zhen) and Guangzhou East train station (Guangzhou Dong Zhan). The former is extremely chaotic and is the main connection point between Guangzhou and the rest of China.

9

In 2008 Guangzhou had four metro lines running. Line one runs from Guangzhou East station in Tianhe district through to the ferry terminal at Nanhai (Pingzhou). Line two operates from north of Guangzhou (Baiyun airport) to the south via the interchange with line one at Gong Yuan Qian. Line three operates from TianHe coach terminal, passes through the city centre and goes to Panyu Square in the south of the city. Line four was opened in the summer of 2007 and operates between JinZhou, in the South-east of Guangzhou, and Wanshengwei (with connections to Line 2). There are further plans for two more lines (line 5 and Line 6) to be opened by 2010, as well as extensions to both Line 2 and Line 3. By the time the Asia Games come to Guangzhou in 2010, all 6 lines should be fully operational.

Metro stations can be identified by a large logo consisting two red lines forming a 'Y' on a yellow or white background. Costs for single trips range from one Yuan to six Yuan depending on the length of the journey.

Sea travel

Guangzhou has a small ferry terminal located in the south-west of the city. The Nanhai port (Pingzhou) has two daily services to central Hong Kong. It takes about two hours and costs approximately 170RMB for a single trip. To get to the ferry terminal you can either take a taxi or the Metro (Line one).

International schools in Guangzhou

American International School of Guangzhou
Box 212, Ti Yu Dong Post Office
Guangzhou, 5106(0)20, China
Tel: +86 (0)20 8735 3393
Fax: +86 (0)20 8735 3339
E-mail: info@aisgz.edu.cn
Website: www.aisgz.edu.cn

British School of Guangzhou
937 Binjiang East Road
Guangzhou

9

Guangdong Province, China
Tel: +86 (0)20 3430 5886
Fax: +86 (0)20 3430 5887
E-mail: info@bsg.org.cn
Website: www.bsg.org.cn

Guangzhou Grace Academy
Riverside Garden, Guangzhou
Guangdong, China
Tel: +86 (0)20 8450 0180
Fax: +86 (0)20 8450 0190
E-mail: ggagga@pub.gz.gd.cn
Website: http://www.ggagga.net/

Guangzhou Nanhu International School
55, Huayang Street
Tiyu Dong Road
TianHe District
Guangzhou, China, 510620
Tel: +86 (0)20 38866952/ 38863606
Fax: +86 38863680
E-mail: admissions@gnischina.com
Website: www.gnischina.com

Utahloy International School
6 km Sha Tai Highway
Jin Bao Gang
Tong He
Guangzhou, 510515, China
Tel: +86 (0)20 8770 3919/3917
Fax: +86 (0)20 8779 1696
E-mail: uis@utahloy.com
Website: www.utahloy.com

Useful Guangzhou links

www.gzmtr.com – Guangzhou metro official website
www.guangzhou.gov.cn – Guangzhou official website
www.gz.gov.cn – Guangzhou (Government) official website
www.destinationprd.com – Information about some cities around the Pearl River Delta
www.thatsgz.com – That's Guangzhou Magazine (Publish monthly)
www.interzum-guangzhou.com – Annual International Trade fair for furniture production

www.lifeofguangzhou.com – Extensive guide to the city

China Foreign Trade Centre
China Foreign Trade Centre (Group)
117 Liuhua Road
Guangzhou, P. R. China
Tel: +86 (0)20 2608 8888
Website: www.cftc.org.cn
Website: www.cantonfair.org.cn

Hong Kong

Many multinationals and Investment banks have their Asia Pacific Head Offices in Hong Kong. One of the world's most cosmopolitan cities; Hong Kong's continued success will increasingly depend on its ability to add value in the economic, social and cultural spheres to meet the needs of its people, the Chinese Mainland and the global market. Hong Kong is seen as a gateway to mainland China by many newcomers to the Chinese market. Others are willing to go for the bigger challenges and bigger rewards by setting up an office in Shanghai or Beijing without going through the Hong Kong route.

9

The next things you notice in Hong Kong, after the multiculturalism, are: the free press (there are numerous publications available here that are prohibited in the mainland), the fashion, the food (even the Chinese food tastes different than in the mainland) and the twenty-four hour hustle and bustle. The general lifestyle of Hong Kong is very appealing, not just to mainland Chinese but also to Asians from other parts of the region. The main drawback is the air pollution, much of which is blown inwards from the industrialised Pearl River delta area.

Hong Kong, like Singapore, has one of the world's biggest and busiest container ports with over 80 per cent of the throughput related to trade directly with China.

Useful Hong Kong websites
www.discoverhongkong.com – Official Tourist website for Hong Kong
www.gov.hk – Official government website of the SAR Hong Kong

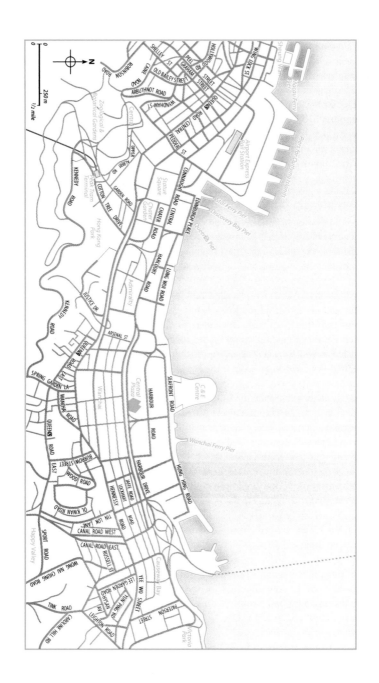

Hong Kong

www.yp.com.hk Hong Kong Yellow Pages
www.explore-hongkong.com – Useful guide for first time visitors
www.hongkong.org – Hong Kong Economic and Trade office in the USA
www.hku.hk – Hong Kong University
www.ust.hk – Hong Kong University of Science and Technology
www.tid.gov.hk – Hong Kong Trade and Industry Department
www.hongkongnews.net – Hong Kong News
www.thestandard.com.hk – Hong Kong English Language Newspaper
www.gohk.gov.hk – Hong Kong Home Affairs department for Tourists

Macau

9

Smaller than Hong Kong (only 26 Sq km in size), Macau is now beginning to attract a large number of tourists. However it is still considered the younger brother to Hong Kong. Macau is famous for gambling and homemade almond butter cookies. The former has been around since licensed gambling was first introduced during the 1850s and these days Macau is being called the Las Vegas of Asia. Macau's casinos are scattered across the region, a peninsula connected to mainland China and two outlying islands called Cotai built on reclaimed land. In August 2007, the world's largest casino, Venetian Casino, managed by the Las Vegas Sands Corporation, officially opened on the island of Cotai. Valued at over $2.4 billion, the Cotai resort contains a hotel with three-thousand rooms, a 15,000-seat sports arena, 1.2 million square feet of convention space, fine dining and room to accommodate six-thousand slot machines as well as eight-hundred gambling tables. Without a doubt there is a lot of money here and every day a considerable number of Chinese from the mainland and Hong Kong come to fill its many casinos in search of fortune. Don't expect to find many James Bond type characters with Tuxedos in these casinos; the majority of gamblers tend to be retired pensioners who are just whiling away time and enjoying the company of fellow senior citizens.

There are a sizeable number of expats from Canada, America and some European nationals who are investing in the Casino business. They have effectively made Macau their second home because of this. Aside from gambling and almond cookies, Macau is also famous for the Grand Prix (both motorbike and car) which is held annually in this beautiful city.

Useful Macau websites

www.macautourism.gov.mo Official Macau Government website
www.wtc-macau.com Macau World Trade Centre
www.macaunews.net Macau News
www.cityguide.gov.mo Macau City Guide
www.umac.mo University of Macau
www.yp.com.mo/en/ Macau Yellow Pages
www.wtc-macau.com – Macau World Trade Centre

Shanghai

Shanghai has had a rich history that has fuelled its success up till today. Like other great non-capital cities around the world, such as Mumbai or New York, Shanghai has become a financial hub of its country. Foreign businesses have always been attracted to Shanghai because of its history as an international city right from the very beginning.

The city is home to one of the largest shipping ports in the world, along with other great marvels of industry that it displays to the world, such as the fastest magnetically operated Maglev train (which travels at a speed of approximately 400Km/h and takes just under 7 minutes to get from the city centre to Pudong Airport).

Surprising as it may seem today, in history this beautiful city used be known by the nickname 'the Paris of the East' because of its neon lights and extravagant nightlife, which included theatre and opera. Foreigners used to have a separate 'international settlement' which protected them from the dirt of everyday life Shanghai. Even today it is amazing to see how the filthy rich live side by side with the filthy poor in Shanghai.

Shanghai

While not as actively industrialised as Guangzhou or Shenzhen, Shanghai does, nevertheless, possess the means to manufacturing and industrial success which have made it an example to other cities in China. At one point in recent times, Shanghai was described as looking like Manchester or Europe after the war, with all the cranes and the rapid pace of building new infrastructure. Across the Huang Pu river, Pudong has seen a dramatic increase in high-rise architecture within the last 10 years. Before that, as you will see if you compare maps from now and then, it was just open land with a few villages. HSBC, ARM Technologies, CSR Technologies and many Investment banks have set up their China head offices in Shanghai (Pudong Area), moving away from cities such as Beijing or even Hong Kong because they realise the potential market that is set to grow even more.

9

Geography

Shanghai (the name means 'Over the sea') is classed as a province itself, known as Shanghai Shi Province. It is flanked by Jiangsu province to the west/north-west and Zhejiang province to the west/south-west. The eastern side of Shanghai is surrounded by Hangzhou Bay to the south and by the mouth of the Yangzi River (which flows into the East China Sea) to the north-east.

Climate

Winters are bitterly cold while the summers are hot and humid. The best time to visit Shanghai is either around April or May when the weather is neither too cold nor too hot, or between August and September when again the weather is mildly cold as it creeps towards the bitter, freezing Shanghai winter.

9

Transportation
Buses and coaches

Shanghai has numerous bus connections operating all around the city during the day and a few at night time. Most buses run from early in the morning (around five o clock) to 11pm.

Air travel

Shanghai has two major international airports, HongQiao and Pudong. Pudong is the international airport located 45km to the east of the city, while HongQiao is much smaller and is located 15km west of the city. In 2008, over sixty international, domestic and cargo airlines operated through Pudong airport and about forty airlines from HongQiao.

Taxies

The minimum fare is eleven Yuan (US$1.38), which covers the first three kilometres, and then two Yuan is charged for every additional kilometre. After ten kilometres, the fare jumps fifty percent – to three Yuan for every additional kilometre.

Trains and metro

Shanghai has two train stations; Shanghai station is north of the Suzhou creek. The station has several routes connecting with other Chinese cities. The other is Shanghai west station, which is situated remotely to the north-west of the city.

Shanghai has one of China's largest metro systems with nine metro lines running across the city by the end of 2007. The government has ambitious plans to extend the number of lines eventually to 18 by 2015!

Shanghai Stock Exchange

The Shanghai Stock Exchange (SSE) became fully operational on 19 December 1990. It is a non-profit-making membership institution directly governed by the China Securities Regulatory Commission (CSRC). By the end of 2007, there were a total of 886 quoted companies listed, including 54 with B-Shares and 832 with A-Shares. An internet link to the SSE is provided at the end of this section.

SSE

9

International schools in Shanghai

British International school of Shanghai

600 Cambridge Forest New Town
2729 Hunan Road
Pudong, Shanghai
201315, China
Tel: +86 (0)21 5812 7455
Fax: +86 (0)21 5812 7465
E-mail: principal@bisshanghai.com
Website: www.bisshanghai.com

Concordia International School (PK-12)
999 Ming Yue Road
JinQiao
Pudong, Shanghai 201206
US style teaching curriculum with a Christian emphasis
Estimated tuition and fees US$12,700-$(0)21,300
Tel: +86 (0)21 5899 0380
Fax: +86 (0)21 5899 1685
E-mail: roberth@ciss.com.cn
Web-Site: www.ciss.com.cn

Dulwich College International – Shanghai (Nursery – Year 9)
Dulwich College Shanghai is a franchise of the famous English public school with its main site in Dulwich, London.
266 LanAn Road, JinQiao, Pudong
Shanghai 201206, China
Tel: +86 (0)21 5899 9910
Website: www.dulwichcollege.cn
E-mail: info@dulwichcollege.cn
Estimated tuition: US$2,600 – $21,400

Deutsche Schule Shanghai (German School of Shanghai)
Together with the French School (EFS) the German School Shanghai (DSS) will build a new and innovative "Eurocampus" for about 1,000 students near HongQiao Airport, due to be completed by summer 2005.
German School of Shanghai
30 Zhu Guang Lu, Lane 399
Shanghai 201702, China
Tel: +86 (0)21 3976 0555
E-mail: info@ds-shanghai.org.cn
Website: www.ds-shanghai.org.cn

Ecole Francaise de Shanghai (3yr – 18yr) (French School of Shanghai)
Located near Hong Qiao airport, the Shanghai French school shares its campus with the Shanghai German School.
30 Zhu Guang Lu, Lane 399
Shanghai 201702
Tel: +86 (0)21 3976 0555
Fax: +86 (0)21 3976 0577
Estimated tuition: $3,000 - $12,000
Website: http://ef.shanghai.online.fr/
E-mail: rm.marchais@ef-shanghai.com

Shanghai American School – Puxi Campus (PK-12)
258 Jin Feng Lu
Zhudi Town, Minhang District
Shanghai, China 201107
Tel: +86 (0)21 6221 1445
Fax: +86 (0)21 6221 1269
E-mail: info@saschina.org
Website: www.saschina.org

9

Puxi Elementary School: http://www.saschina.org/es
Puxi Middle School: www.saschina.org/sams
Puxi High School: www.saschina.org/hs
Accepts English speaking students
Estimated tuition and fees US$11,500-$22,800

Shanghai American School – PuDongCampus (PK-8)
Shanghai Links Executive Community
San Jia Gang, Pudong
Shanghai, China 201201
Tel: +86 (0)21 6221 1445
Fax: +86 (0)21 5897 0011
E-mail: info@saschina.org
Pudong School: http://www.saschina.org/pudong/
Accepts English speaking students
Estimated tuition and fees US$11,500-$22,800

Shanghai Community International Schools (PK-12)
Web-Site: www.scischina.org
E-mail: info@scischina.org
Pudong campus
800 Xiuyan Road
Kangqiao, Pudong
Shanghai, China 201315
Tel: +86 (0)21 5812 9888
Fax: +86 (0)21 5812 9000

HongQiao Campus
1161 Hongqiao Road
Shanghai, China 200051
US-based educational program in a small school
environment.
Estimated tuition and fees US$8,000-$20,000
Tel: +86 (0)21 6261 4338
Fax: +86 (0)21 6261 4639

Shanghai Japanese School
3185 Hongmei Road, Hong Qiao
Japanese nationals only
Fees: approx. 80,000 Japanese yen per month.
The school has over 700 Japanese students, tuition fees
for primary and middle school are RMB 1,200 per month.
Tel: +86 (0)21 6401 2747
Fax: +86 (0)21 6401 2747

9

Shanghai Korean School
2999 Qi Xin Road
Korean nationals only

Shanghai Livingston American School (PK-12)
Curriculum and instruction are modeled on the
California public school system.
Estimated tuition: $11,000 - $18,500
580 GanXi Rd
ChangNing District
Shanghai 200336, CHINA
Tel: +86 (0)21 6238 3511/5218 8372
Fax: +86 (0)21 5218 0390
Website: www.laschina.org
E-mail: info@laschina.org

Shanghai Rego International School
189 Dongzha Road
Minhang District
Shanghai 201100
Tel: +86 (0)21 6492 3431
Fax: +86 (0)21 6498 5072
E-mail: info@srisrego.com
Website: www.srisrego.com

Shanghai Singapore International School
301, Zhujian Road
MinHang District
Shanghai P.R.C. 201107
Tel: +86 (0)21 62219288
Fax: +86 (0)21 62219188
Website: www.ssis.cn

Sino-Canada High School
1 Liannan Rd
Luxu Town Wujiang
Suzhou, Jiangsu Province
China, 215211
Tel: +86 (0)512 63262288
Fax: +86 (0)512 63262255
E-mail: info@sinocanada.cn
Website: www.sinocanada.cn

SMIC Private School (PK-12)
Semiconductor Manufacturing International Cooperation
School
169 Qing-Tong Road
Pudong 201203
Tel: +86 (0)21 5855 4588, ext.230
Website: www.smic-school.cn
E-mail: Gregory_Jones@smicschool.com
English and Chinese track courses.
Currently has more then 500 students and 90 faculty
members.
Estimated tuition: $6,000 – $9,000

**Western International School of Shanghai, – International
School (American Curriculum)**
555 Lian Min Road
Xujing Town, Qing Pu District
Shanghai, PRC 201702
Tel: +86 (0)21 6976 6388, 6976 6969
Fax: +86 (0)21 6976 6833
E-mail: admission@wiss.cn
Website: www.wiss.cn

9

Useful links
www.thatssh.com – Monthly guide of Shanghai for
expats.
www.shanghai-ed.com – Website for expats
www.shanghaiexpat.com – Website for expats in Shanghai
www.shanghaidaily.com – Online edition of the Shanghai
English news paper
www.shanghai.gov.cn – Official Government portal
of Shanghai
www.portshanghai.com.cn – Official website for the sea
ports in Shanghai
www.f1china.com.cn – The official website for the
Shanghai Formula One Grand Prix
www.expo2010china.com – The official website for the
World Expo in Shanghai in 2010.
www.smtdc.com – The official website for the Shanghai
Maglev train
www.shtmetro.com – The official website for the
Shanghai metro (is in Chinese)
www.sse.com.cn – Shanghai Stock Exchange –
official website

Shenzhen

Having been formally established in November 1979, Shenzhen is considered to be China's youngest, cleanest and most modern city and is nicknamed 'China's Garden City'. Shenzhen is a sister city of Bangalore, India (as Bangalore is also known as a 'Garden City' and also attracts a large number of foreign workers).

Shenzhen was a simple fishing village until Deng Xiao Ping declared the city as a Special Economic Zone (SEZ), along with four other Chinese cities on the east coast between 1980 and 1984. It is known as China's garden city because of its abundance of greenery and flower beds scattered on almost every roadside. Shenzhen will probably surprise you if this is the first city you come to on you inaugural trip to China. People from the west have usually never heard of it. Hong Kong media will tell you that it is the most dangerous place in China and the Taiwanese and Japanese think that it is some poor cousin of Shanghai. Shenzhen is actually a city of some eleven million people, with the majority of them migrants from other parts of China as well as overseas. It is also the wealthiest city in China paying the highest average salaries to its inhabitants.

Indeed Shenzhen is China's migrant city where people from other parts of China have come to seek an opportunity, and it provides a sense of freedom for the younger population.

The majority of the expatriate community resides about 30km west of the city centre in the port area known as Shekou (Close to Nanshan District), with most of the expats who live there, working within the Oil, Gas or Semiconductor industries. Multinationals such as Siemens, Philips Electronics, Conocophillips, BP as well as over 700 other International companies (SME and large multinationals) have established their offices, R&D or manufacturing facilities in the Shekou Area or the Nanyou Da Sha Industrial Park in Nanshan District of Shenzhen. This figure is set to grow in the next 10 to 15 years as there is a huge amount of attention being paid to Shenzhen and China on the whole. Many companies are relocating from Guangzhou, Wuxi or other parts of China to Shenzhen because of its proximity to Hong Kong.

9

Shenzhen is also host to a wide range of international exhibitions, forums and conferences. For companies hosting an exhibition Shenzhen provides a cheaper alternative and be convenient for dignitaries visiting for one or two day trips from Hong Kong. In 2007, there were over 150 exhibitions, forums and conferences held in the areas around Shenzhen. Wuzhou guest house (www.wuzhouguesthouse.com) is a five star hotel in Nanshan district that also acts as a conference hall for political figures and senior executives from large multinationals.

Geography

Shenzhen is located in Guangdong province, SE China, on the border of Hong Kong. Shenzhen covers an area of approximately 2020 Sq km and is made up of five main districts, Lowu, Longgang, Futian, Nanshan and Baoan. Lowu and Futian border Hong Kong; there are three main border entry points with Hong Kong, the main one being at Lowu Train Station and the other two at Huanggang and Shekou seaport. Two more border crossings were opened in 2008.

9

Dongguan and Chang An

From Shenzhen to Guangzhou it takes about an hour by high speed train or about ninety minutes by non-stop air-conditioned coach. The whole route between Shenzhen and Guangzhou is lined up with factories that churn out 'Made in China' goods that get exported world-wide. About halfway between Shenzhen and Guangzhou is the city of Dongguan, which is connected with the Shenzhen Special Economic Zone (SEZ). Within Dongguan is the Chung An Industrial Town, and this has become very popular among multinationals as a haven for foreign investment. You will see building after building with large 'ISO 9001 Quality' banners on them. At one point in 2006, a local expat publication pointed out that there are over 2,500 foreign enterprises in the Chang An area alone, of which around 60 per cent are from Hong Kong – the others belonging to Japanese, US, Taiwanese and Korean companies.

While I was working as an expatriate in Shenzhen, I was told that over ninety per cent of the world's DVD players are manufactured at just one factory in Dongguan; and that with most of the products the only difference is that they are branded differently according to the company that supplies the licence.

Climate

Shenzhen's climate is blessed with the mixed characteristics of tropical and subtropical zones. Shenzhen experiences long summers that range from around February until October. During the months between April and September there is a high percentage of precipitation. Winter is short and surprisingly very cold (normally experienced for about one or two months around December and January).

9

Transportation

Buses

Shenzhen has numerous bus connections operating all around the city during the day and a few night buses as well. Long distance coaches operate from the main train station at Lowu and also from Futian Bus Station.

Air travel

Shenzhen has one major international airport. Bao'an International airport is located 32km to the north-west of the city centre, near the Pearl Delta, with connections to major Asian cities as well as many domestic flights. Shenzhen has its own airline, Shenzhen Airlines, with numerous daily flights to destinations within China and several Asian cities. In 2007, Shenzhen Bao'an airport handled an estimated 18 million passengers and over thirty airlines operated from the airport.

Taxies

Metered taxies are available 24 hours a day. The base rate at the time of writing is 12.50RMB (Approx $1.50) between 06:00am and 11:00pm for the first mile. Between 11:00pm and 06:00am the base rate is 16.50RMB (just over $2). Inside the city centre (Special Economic Zone) the taxies are coloured Red, while those operating outside the city are coloured Green.

Ferry travel

The main port for travelling by ferry is Shekou. Destinations include Hong Kong (Central and Kowloon), Macau, Hong Kong Airport, Guangzhou and Zhuhai. At the time of writing the standard fare for going to Hong Kong airport (Should take approx thirty minutes) is HK$250 (You will get about HK$150 refund if you show your flight ticket at check-in).

Trains and metro

Shenzhen has many routes connecting other Chinese cities. The most frequently operated route is the Guangzhou to Shenzhen route, trains run every twenty to twenty-five minutes with some trains stopping in Dongguan. The trip takes approximately one hour. The one way fare at the time of writing is 70RMB.

Shenzhen Metro opened in December 2005. Trains are not as crowded as one would experience in other Chinese cities. At the time of writing there are two lines (Line one and Line four) open. There are three more lines set to be in full operation by 2010.

9

Accommodation

At the end of 2008, it was listed that Shenzhen has over 220 hotels of all different quality and size. This number is set to grow in time. A list of some good hotels in Shenzhen is provided in Appendix 1.

Shenzhen Stock Exchange

Located in the Lowu district of Shenzhen, Shenzhen Stock Exchange (the SSE) is a national stock exchange under the China Securities Regulatory Commission (the CSRC). It was established in 1990, the same year as Shanghai Stock Exchange. In 2008, the Shenzhen Stock Exchange had over 540 listed companies, 35 million registered investors and 177 exchange members. On average, on a daily basis, around 600,000 deals (valued at US$ 807 million) trade on the SSE. The main website for the Shenzhen Stock Exchange is listed at the end of this section.

Shekou International School
Jing Shan Villas, Nan Hai Road, Shekou, Shenzhen
Guangdong Province 518067
People's Republic of China
Te: +86 (0)755 2669 3669
Fax: +86 (0)755 2667 4099
E-mail: sis@sis.org.cn
E-mail: admissions@sis.org.cn
Website: www.sis.org.cn

QSI International School of Shenzhen (Shekou)
2nd Floor, Bitao Building
8 Tai Zi Road, Shekou
Shenzhen, Guangdong, China 518069
Tel: +86 (0)755 2667 6030/ +86 (0)755 2667 6031
E-mail: Shenzhen@qsi.org
E-mail: Shekou@qsi.org

9

Useful Shenzhen Links

www.sznews.com/szdaily – Shenzhen Daily is the main
English daily tabloid
ww.shenzhenparty.com – The "What's happening" guide
for expats in Shenzhen
www.shenzhenwindow.net
www.szftz.gov.cn/sze/index.htm – Shenzhen
Administrative Bureau of Free Trade Zones
http://english.sz.gov.cn/lis/ – Shenzhen Government Online
www.destinationprd.com – Website detailing some of the
cities around the Pearl River Delta.
www.missionhillsgroup.com – Official website of the
Mission Hills Golf Club
www.szwwco.com – Window of the World attraction-
Official website
www.szmc.net – Shenzhen Metro Website
www.heliexpress.com – The website for Heli Express-
based at Shenzhen Airport.
www.sz2011.org – Shenzhen Universiade 2011 official
website
www.szse.cn – Shenzhen Stock Exchange- official website

Shenzhen High-Tech Industrial Park
3F Virtual University
P.R.C 518057
www.ship.gov.cn/en/index.htm

Western China

The western region of China, which includes cities such as Chongqing, Sichuan (formally with the capital, Chengdu), Yunnan and Guizhou as well as the regions of Tibet, Xinjiang, Guangxi and Inner Mongolia, has a combined population of approximately 400 million. It is a land that is full of opportunity, therefore businesses cannot afford to turn a blind eye to this part of China. As of the end of 2007, a total of over 1 trillion Yuan has been spent building infrastructure in western China including the first metro line for the city of Chongqing that was opened in 2006, with a further 3 more metro lines planned to be open by 2010 in order to ease the severe traffic congestion in the teeming city centre everyday. Chongqing is a sister city to Leicester (UK) as well as Detroit and Seattle in the US. In 2008, the population of Chongqing was a staggering 35 million and this should not come as a surprise because it is China's largest city. The city is famous for many things including Red Rock Village Museum, which is the official former home of Mao Zedong and Zhou Enlai. They both lived here during the revolution years.

9

Chongqing is also home to spicy Sichuan cuisine. Apart from these, the main reason for being attracted to Chongqing is that it is an industrial honey pot for foreign investors. Foreign businesses that have firmly established themselves in the city include the following:

- Oil Companies (BP, Sinopac and Conocophillips are a few examples)
- Food and confectionary products (The former is not a huge industry in China but business in the chocolate industry is gradually picking up, with Mars and Cadbury's setting up subsidiary plants in China in recent years).
- Pharmaceutical companies. In addition to well known brands such as GSK, Pfizer and Astra Zeneca, there are also Chinese companies that are forging links with these companies such as 'Jumpcan Pharmaceutical' (www.jumpcan.com).
- Construction companies and consultants (Bechtel is an excellent example)
- International Banks
- International Hotel Chains

- Management Consultancies (a list is provided in Chapter 2)
- Building Material Suppliers

In winter 2007, the Chinese government gave the green light for Chongqing and Chengdu to merge together to make up a new, twin-city special economic zone (SEZ). This is a move to encourage the expansion of this economically poorer but 'full of opportunity' region of the country. China's western region has reported an annual average economic growth rate of approximately eleven per cent for the last six years in a row. The combined GDP of western regions reached over four trillion Yuan in 2007, compared with 1.66 trillion Yuan in 2000, while net income grew on average twelve per cent for urban residents in the west and just over seven per cent for rural residents. For further details about business or travel plans as a delegation to Chongqing or Chengdu, please contact your Chamber of Commerce or Consulate-general (Lists provide in Chapter 2 and in Appendix 1).

9

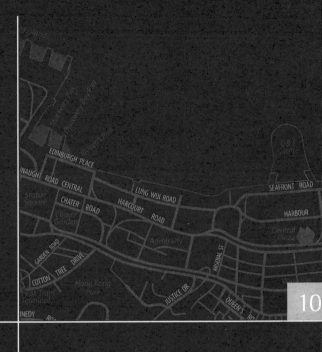

a break from business

10

a break from business

10

Things to do and see in some
cities within China, Hong Kong
and Macau

Places of interest in Guangzhou

Like many cities in China, Guangzhou has quite a number of beautiful parks. Here is a description of some of the major attractions for the visitor.

Yuexiu Park (Yuexiu Gong Yuan) is located in downtown Guangzhou and has entrances on all four roads that surround the park. The main entrance is located on Jiefeng Lu and leads the visitor up the hill to the Five Rams Statue. The 'five rams' is the official symbol of Guangzhou because according to local myths the city was founded by five immortals riding five rams.

Sun Yat Sen memorial Hall (Sun Zhongshan Jiniantang) – A grand theatre located in a large square park between Dongfeng Zhong Lu and Qingyun Lu (facing Yuexiu Park). It is host to quite a number of foreign Orchestras and Opera shows.

Six Banyan Trees Temple (Liurong Si) – Located on Liurong Lu to the south of Yuexiu Park; this beautiful temple dates back to the fifth century and is considered older than the city itself. You can climb to the top of the pagoda in the middle of the courtyard; however, as more buildings are being constructed around the temple area, the views are not as beautiful as they once were.

10

Food and shopping in Guangzhou

Guangzhou has attracted traders and businesses people for thousands of years. The city is no stranger to the curious 'businessman turned tourist' who asks too many questions about the price or quality of a product that tickles his fancy. All year round in Guangzhou, it is easy to observe eager traders and businessmen wandering around exhibition halls and shopping malls like kids in a candy shop in search of the product with which they can say 'Eureka! I can make millions selling this back in my homeland!'.

In terms of food, there is a wide variety for foreigners to choose from. Guangzhou's restaurants cater for all tastes and cultures. There are authentic restaurants that belong to Turkish, Muslim (from Xinjiang and Central Europe), Middle-Eastern, Italian, Kenyan, Indian and Pakistani communities. There is even a British style pub (**Elephant & Castle Bar** located near the Baiyun Hotel on Huanshi Dong Lu). The Malaysian chain restaurants, **Banana Leaf Restaurant** is quite a popular place for many foreigners, where live musicians from the Philippines and Indonesia play romantic melodies while you tuck in to your Coconut flavoured Chicken Curry!

Guangzhou has many areas for shopping, with both authentic and fake goods on offer. There is an area to the north of the city centre (Xiaobei Lu, an inconspicuous road located in the Yuexiu district of Guangzhou), that is home to Guangzhou's African and Middle Eastern communities (mostly from Nigeria, Ethiopia, Egypt and Kenya). The area makes you feel as though you are suddenly in Africa or downtown Cairo because there are a large number of African and Arab traders involved in the shoe, mobile phone and fabric industry. Ventures here give the impression that many of the branded products on offer are not genuine. Nevertheless, many foreign business people come to this part of the city to do bulk shopping for all kinds of products to then export to Europe, Africa and the Americas.

Like Beijing, Guangzhou has its own **Friendship store**. Located in a five story building on Huanshi Dong Lu, this is a good place to go for souvenirs and gifts as well as designer goods and houshold appliances.

Beijing Road (**Beijing Lu**) – Guangzhou's busiest street houses many interesting shops and restaurants. There are many small shops selling watches, jade and other ornaments. There are also numerous opticians, dentists and small malls that have shops selling just about anything you can imagine. It's a busy place at any time of the week; irrespective of how good or bad the weather is, people come and shop or just visit the road because it's one of the main attractions for tourists. **Citic Plaza Mall** (Huanshi Dong Lu) and **White Swan Arcade** (Shamian Island) are also popular with expats.

Places of interest in Hong Kong

Hong Kong is an exotic place with many tourist attractions available to choose from. If you want to get away from the hustle and bustle of the City centre then there are a whole range of other pleasures that you can indulge in around the many islands, with their beautiful white sandy beaches, picturesque temples, and mountains and hills for walking and admiring the spectacular views.

Then there is **Hong Kong Disney Land** on LanTau Island, which is rather smaller in size than Disneyland in Paris or the US – but nevertheless offers the same excitement and joy for both adults and children in watching some amazing shows that will leave you wanting to come back again and again! A full day would be required to absorb everything the park has to offer.

Ocean Park: This is a large theme park (Hong Kong's answer to UK's Alton Towers) which features some spectacular shows with pandas, dolphins dancing, other animals on display plus an aquarium. It's a park suitable for both adults and children.

Nathan Road and Jordan: Both of these areas in Kowloon are classed as the most happening places in this part of Hong Kong for clubbing, shopping and eating. There are myriad restaurants and shops ranging from jwellery, fabrics and designer clothes to electronic products. Be aware of fakes and bystanders offering you 'Special offers' on Rolex/Armani etc! Apart from the usual renowned designer wear shops, there are quite a number of foreign brand stores as well, such as Marks & Spencer's (UK), Body Shop (UK) and Carrefour (France) to name just a few.

Jade Market: This is located in Yau Ma Tei, Kowloon where there are approximately 500 stalls selling nothing but genuine Jade of all sizes, shapes and quality. It is open daily from 10.30am till 3.30pm. Even though Jade is very important to all Chinese, it is especially important here in Hong Kong because Hong Kong is the world's top jade trading centre.

The Peak (on Hong Kong Island): Even if it is not a clear day, a visit to the Victoria Peak, at 552m above sea level, is a must for any new comer to Hong Kong. It is best at

10

night, when the lights in the city add to the romance and exotica of the place. The famous Peak Tram runs from Garden Road in Central on the steep mountain, passing by some really exquisite properties and buildings that are located on the slope, every day from 7am until midnight. The views from the Peak Tower (at 396m) and from the Peak Galleria shopping Plaza are truly breathtaking.

The Star Ferry: For all tourists to Hong Kong, this is a must as part of their touring package. The Star Ferry is a convenient and cost effective way to get from Central to Kowloon, and well worth while for the amazing views offered of Hong Kong's skyline on both sides of the harbour. It only costs about $3 HKD for a one way ride and takes about five to ten minutes to cross the harbour between Central and Kowloon. In 2007 there was a new pier established for the Star Ferry on the Kowloon side, making it more convenient for passengers boarding the ferry there.

Because Hong Kong is on the border to China, it is convenient to visit for a one or two day excursion. Hong Kong's slogan is 'Asia's World City' and this statement is most certainly true considering the multi-cultural environment. This gives the place a good mix of East and West. There are restaurants offering all kinds of international cuisine. A useful website to check out for food in Hong Kong is: www.hongkongfoodguide.com

Places of interest in Macau

Macau's three islands have many beautiful Churches, Temples, homes with Portuguese architecture and, of course, Casinos! Plus there are scores of cycling and walking routes in and around the islands. You can climb up the **Macau Tower** to get some stunning views of the country, Zhuhai in China and, on a clear day, Hong Kong as well. It rises to a staggering 381 meters and is currently ranked the tenth tallest tower in the world.

On the southern Island, Coloane, there are a number of clean beaches, such as **Cheoc Van** and **Hac Sa**. Both are relatively easy to get by either bike or bus and would provide a good day out and a lovely picnic spot.

10

Places of interest in Shanghai

Contrary to the preconception that foreigners have of Shanghai because of its beauty and history, the city itself isn't really classed as a tourist destination. It is, after all, China's financial capital, so its presence is regarded more for working purposes. Here are a few sights the business tourist may enjoy seeing.

The Shanghainese people consider the **Oriental Pearl Television Tower (Dongfang Minzhu)** to be the main symbol of the city – before it was built people used to identify Shanghai (and still do to some extent) by the bend of the road where the old HSBC Head Office and Peace Hotel are situated on the Bund. The Pearl Tower is made up of eleven steel spheres of different sizes that are supposed to represent pearls, with the top 'pearl' offering a 360-degree view of the surroundings. The name of the tower derives from the phrase 'Shanghai – Pearl of the East'.

The Pearl River Promenade – The waterfront avenue, more formally known as the Bund (Wai-tan) used to be known as Shanghai's symbolic landmark (and still is by some people as mentioned above). During the Pre-Second World War era, Europeans and other foreigners built their banks, clubs, hotels and consulates here. The Bund is now a busy place for both tourists and residents at all times of the day, and even more so in the evenings. The historic buildings have been beautifully renovated, restoring the glory of their original architecture.

Places of interest in Shenzhen

Window of the world is Shenzhen's star attraction; it features the world's wonders, historic sites, scenic spots, natural landscapes, folk customs and world renowned sculptures. Occupying an area of almost forty-eight hectares, it is composed of 118 attractions set up on different scales from 1:1 to 1:100 including the UK Houses of Parliament, The White House and the Sydney Opera House.

Happy Valley is an amusement park with a lot of attractions for both adults and children. Consisting of a water park and a dry park, it features attractions for

10

both adults and children's. The park also has a 4D cinema, the fist of its kind in Asia.

Splendid China and the China Folk Cultural Village are both located adjacent to the Windows of the World. 'Splendid China' features detailed replicas of many of the most famous historic buildings in China built, for the most part, to 1:15 scale and positioned according to their geographical location. Alongside these replicas are over 50,000 ceramic figures and exhibits representing folk customs. This is a wonderful place to reflect on China and its five-thousand years of history and culture that are waiting to be absorbed by visitors.

Shenzhen has a number of golf courses which are popular with people from Hong Kong who come over for the weekend to play here. The most famous venue is the **Mission Hills Golf course**. It is expensive even for China, but it caters to a very affluent market and is worthy of its status.

Food and shopping in Shenzhen

Shenzhen does not possess the large choice of restaurants and International cuisine that you will find in Guangzhou, Shanghai or Hong Kong; however there is a sound selection of restaurants on offer. A good place to find restaurants is the Shenzhen party website (a link is given towards at the end of this section). A number of Western style restaurants (mainly Indian and Italian) are available in the Lowu area, while the MixC centre, opposite The Diwang building on Shen Nan Zhong Lu, has an abundance of Chinese, Japanese and western style restaurants including 'Taco Bell' (Mexican) and 'Spaghetti House' (Italian). During your stay you should be sure to try one of the many local eateries in the Lowu part of the city.

Here are some of the best shopping centres in Shenzhen:

Dongmen in Lowu district – a bustling and vibrant shopping area in the heart of Shenzhen's most happening neighbourhood.

10

Hua Qiang Bei in Futian District – Similar to Dongmen but specializing in 'Made in Shenzhen' electronic goods.

The MixC is a new shopping centre, located opposite the Diwang Building (Shenzhen's tallest building in the heart of the city) on Shennan Road. The MixC is a modern shopping mall with all kinds of restaurants including one of China's three Taco Bell outlets (the other two are in Shanghai), and a French Supermarket catering to the expat community with imported goods (Ole). The MixC is also home to many other stores with familiar names, a huge indoor ice rink and a cinema.

Other activities in China

According to the China National Tourism Administration, in 2007 there were approximately 16,000 natural, cultural and man-made places of interest. There are plenty of open air and indoor swimming pools which you can go to. Most real estate developments have their own in-house gym and swimming facilities that can be used by the residents for a minute cost compared to public facilities. Parks in China have a small entrance charge, normally approximately three Yuan, and it is worth it!

10

Every major city and town in China has numerous beautiful parks and lakes. These parks are kept clean and have a small entrance fee. China is a country with over 2,500 natural lakes with total area more than 80,000 square kilometers. Some of the more popular parks and lakes have traditional Chinese instrumental music being played, normally with the recorded sound of a 'Zheng', an eight or twenty five plucked string instrument. The speakers are camouflaged in shrubs and flowers. Public parks are extremely congested during the holiday season with families, tour groups and couples.

In twenty-first century China, the average Chinese family spends quite a lot of money on enjoying themselves by going on holiday to other parts of China or even abroad. This may seem normal to westerners, but before 1979 hardly any Chinese people went on holiday anywhere – just a stroll to the local park or the opera would have been sufficient. But rising salaries and more holidays (especially for those working in foreign multinationals and diplomatic missions), have created a chance for Chinese people to treat themselves and enjoy their lives to the full – an ethos of 'work hard and play hard' has been created, as opposed to just the 'work hard' philosophy of the Mao years. Some Chinese people are spending even more than westerners on holidays each year and this is set to continue into the future with the rising economy.

Apart from the sightseeing, a journey to China would be wasted if you did not experience some of the things that Chinese people do in their spare time for entertainment.

Chinese Opera

Even though most foreigners are familiar with the famous Beijing Opera, Chinese opera also comes in various other styles, such as Cantonese Opera from Guangzhou and Sichuan Opera.

10

Chinese Opera is one of the major attractions and is a must to see! No trip to Guangdong should go by without seeing Cantonese Opera at the local theatre. The same goes for Beijing (Or Peking Opera as some people call it!). The experience is something special, and if you love the costumes and the high pitched singing then it is an ideal thing to do in your spare time after work. Don't worry about the language barrier; even most native Chinese people don't understand what the actors say when performing the shows! Tickets can be very expensive during the holiday season and, in touristy places like Beijing, almost all shows are fully booked. Some theatres in Guangzhou even sell special discount tickets for group bookings during the trade shows. All theatres in China are clean, spacious and have some facility for refreshments (Chinese refreshments such as instant noodles, green tea, boiled eggs in Soya Sauce and other savouries).

KTV Bars

KTV is short for Karaoke, and the Chinese people, primarily the younger generation but many corporate professionals too, love to spend the evenings after a stressful day at work singing with their friends. KTV rooms have a television in the middle of the room. There is usually a selection of nuts and savouries as well as ordered alcoholic and non-alcoholic drinks. It is a great party atmosphere but can be rather boring for foreigners as there are rarely many songs in English (and if there are any they might not be your cup of tea!). Your colleagues will probably take you to a nice KTV bar if you wish to go.

Massage

Massage is a popular pastime in all Asian countries and nowhere is it more popular than in Greater China. There are massage parlours all over Hong Kong, Macau and China. Although in the latter you have to be careful which places you venture into, as many are actually illegal brothels in disguise; sometimes as massage parlours and sometimes even as the numerous 'hair salons' in all the cities in mainland China. Usually you can tell the difference because the staff members at a genuine massage parlour wear a uniform (usually a traditional 'Qi piao') and a lot less make-up!

Those that are genuine, and in Hong Kong most are, offer a good and safe service with professional staff. You can have a head, body or foot massage, manicure, pedicure, sauna, and steam or plunge bath. Men and Women customers are usually in separate areas, although for foot massage or head massage this doesn't matter and it's good to relax with your friends, and maybe drink Chinese tea.

Ballroom dancing and salsa

The Chinese people love dancing as a pastime. In the morning in any city you will normally see elderly people dancing slowly, with the women holding traditional Chinese fans and the men holding umbrellas that may also symbolise swords.

In the evenings you will often see couples in parks, or the elderly dancing to loud and erratic sounding music that is sometimes completely out of tune! On a few occasions I was surprised to hear Hindi pop music being played loudly while middle-aged Chinese couples danced in a

10

style similar to ball room dancing – I am sure they didn't have a clue what kind of music was being played but they definitely seemed to enjoy it!

Increasingly the younger Chinese generation has taken to learning western dance styles such as Salsa. Most major cities, including Shanghai and Shenzhen, have expatriates who teach Chinese people Salsa dancing or Indian dancing in the evenings. These classes are usually advertised in expat magazines or websites.

Drinking tea in tea houses

The Chinese people drink large quantities of 'green tea', which is normally drunk without adding sugar or milk (some people prefer to add Honey instead). Fresh processed tea leaves can be bought as souvenirs at special tea shops in most cities. You can normally sit down and taste the different kinds of tea before deciding if you want to buy it. Tea shops are colourful with nice decorations and beautifully coloured wooden boxes in which you can keep the whole set of tea utensils, such as a small tea pot along with tea cups.

Small amounts of fresh tea leaves are mixed with boiled water and require about five minutes to infuse before you start drinking. Drinking Chinese tea can be tricky, especially if there are a lot of large tea leaves getting in the way of your mouth when sipping from the large mugs that people drink from. This is the reason why Chinese tea mugs have a lid to push away the leaves when you sip the fresh tea.

Tea houses (Cha-dian) are places where people can go to relax after a long day at work, usually in groups with friends or colleagues. The experience of going to Tea house is similar to going for a massage or the KTV, its all part of the Chinese way of relaxing after a hard day at work. Tea Houses can also provide a place for possible networking opportunity for colleagues and friends, or to discuss any problems in private away from the office or home.

10

Seafood and Dim Sum

Eating out is a very big part of Chinese life, and going to a restaurant is about more than just eating a meal with your friends. This may not be the case however if you are going for a formal meal at lunchtime when you don't have enough time to indulge in conversations that aren't work related.

On informal occasions when you are dining out with your friends or colleagues in the evenings or at weekends, you will realise that on the table there will usually be lots of fresh or cooked (steamed or grilled) seafood. There is well established superstition within the fishing community that while eating your fish it should never be turned over as this will cause your ship to capsize! True or not, the art of eating a fish with chopsticks is one which you will have to master while in China. It is amazing to see your Chinese counterparts eat even the smallest of bits of food, including grains of rice, or separating the bones in the fish, with just their chopsticks!

Dim Sum is a special part of the daily diet for Cantonese people (Dim Sum originates in Guangdong Province, Macau and Hong Kong; but of course is available all over China in selected restaurants and Hotels). Dim Sum is usually served from early morning till the afternoon, with a good Chinese tea such as jasmine tea or any other Green tea.

As in any other restaurant in China, when you are served Dim Sum, the waitress/waiter will bring small servings of various dishes laid on a trolley to your table, and as you choose the various dishes, your bill card is appropriately stamped to indicate what you have ordered and the quantity. This makes it easier for the restaurant staff because usually restaurants in China are very busy – and very noisy too so it is easy to forget what was ordered and by whom!.

Breakfast is the one meal when people most yearn for their native cuisine because it is a comforting part of the routine of getting up. What you will be served for breakfast at your hotel depends on if you are staying in a western style hotel or not. In China breakfast is usually

10

laid out in a nice buffet: for westerners there may be a selection of sliced meats and cheese, good buns or toast, eggs, hash-brown potatoes, sausage, strong coffee and tea, a good selection of cereals and yogurt (usually Danone, because they are main importer of foreign dairy products into China). For the Chinese there usually tend to be a mixture of Sichuan spicy pickles, sushi, cold or hot noodles, steamed buns, dim sum and hot congee cereal.

If you want to have a romantic meal with your loved one then maybe a typical loud Chinese restaurant is not a good venue to treat yourselves! But on the whole eating Dim Sum is wonderful experience and it will touch your taste buds like they have never been touched before!

A typical meal for one in a normal Chinese restaurant should not cost more than 20 to 30RMB. But this is just an indication, as there are restaurants in China that offer a very good and healthy meal for as little as 8RMB (US$1!), while on the other side of the coin you can easily pay a whopping 300RMB per person at a top quality restaurant. It all depends on choice. For example when I was working as an expat for a multinational in Shenzhen, my colleagues used to take us to a different restaurant at lunch time every day, and our meals cost at most 10RMB (this came complete with a drink and salad). In Hong Kong, it is slightly more expensive than the mainland, but on average, a decent meal for one person should cost no more than HK$30.

10

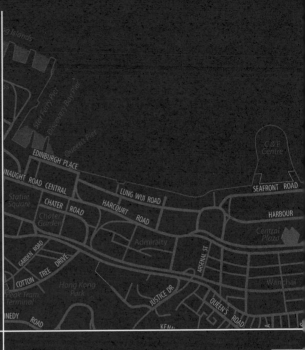

appendix one

A1

appendix one

A directory of useful telephone numbers and contact details.

Emergencies

	PRC	HKG SAR	MACAU SAR
Ambulance	120	999	999
Police	110	999	999
Fire	119	999	999

Tourist Hotline
Tel: +86 (0)65130828   +852 28076177   +853 28333000

Beijing PSB Department www.bjgaj.gov.cn
Tel: +86 (0)10 8402 0101

Hong Kong Police: www.police.gov.hk
Tel: +852 2527 7177

Macau Police: www.pj.gov.mo
Tel: +853 2855 7775/ 2855 7777

Telephone Services

Local Telephone Information	Tel: 114	Tel: 1083
Time Check	Tel: 117	
Weather check	Tel: 121	Tel: 1311
Post code check	Tel: +86 (0)10 6303 7131	

Embassies & Consulate-Generals

	Beijing	Hong Kong
Australia	Tel: +86 (0)10 6532 2331	+852 2827 8881
Canada	Tel: +86 (0)10 6532 3536	+852 3719 4700
Finland	Tel: +86 (0)10 6532 1817	+852 2525 5385
France	Tel: +86 (0)10 6532 1331	+852 2529 4351
Germany	Tel: +86 (0)10 8532 9000	+852 2529 8855
India	Tel: +86 (0)10 6532 1908	+852 2528 4475
Italy	Tel: +86 (0)10 8532 7600	+852 2522 0033
Japan	Tel: +86 (0)10 6532 2361	+852 2522 1184
New Zealand	Tel: +86 (0)10 6532 2731	+852 2525 5044
Russia	Tel: +86 (0)10 6532 2051	+852 2877 7188

A1

Singapore	Tel: +86 (0)10 6532 1115	+852 2527 2212
South Africa	Tel: +86 (0)10 6532 0171	+852 2577 3279
United Kingdom		
	Tel: +86 (0)10 5192 4000	+852 2901 3000
USA	Tel: +86 (0)10 6532 3831	+852 2523 9011

Hospitals & Dentists

For a full list contact your Embassy, Consulate-General of Chamber of Commerce in China

Beijing

Beijing Union Medical Hospital
Tel: +86 (0)10 6529-5284

Beijing United Family Hospital
Tel: +86 (0)10 6433-3960

Beijing International SOS Centre
Tel: +86 (0)10 6462 9100

American-Sino Medical Clinic
Tel: +86 (0)10 6496 8888

Shanghai

Huashan Hospital
Tel: +86 (0)21 6248 9999 ext 1900 (24hr)

Guangzhou

Guangzhou General Military Hospital
Tel: +86 (0)20 8666 2205

Dental Association:

Hong Kong: www.hkda.org   Tel: +852 2528 5327
Shanghai: www.dds-dental.com   Tel: +86 (0)21 5465 2678

Airlines

	Beijing Office	Hong Kong Office
Aeroflot	Tel: +86 (0)10 6501 2563	Tel: +852 2537 2611
Aerosvit Airlines	Tel: +86 (0)10 8458 0909	
Air Astana	Tel: +86 (0)10 6465 1030	

A1

Air Canada
     Tel: +86 (0)10 6468 2001   Tel: +852 2867 8111

Air China
     Tel: +86 (0)10 6459 5912

Air India
     Tel: +852 2522 4772

Air France
     Tel: +86 (0)10 5922 0808   Tel: +852 2501 9433

Air Macau
     Tel: +86 (0)10 6515 8988

Air Mauritius
     Tel: +86 (0)10 6581 2968   Tel: +852 2523 1114

Air New Zealand
     Tel: +852 2862 8988

Air Niugini
     Tel: +852 2527 7098

Alitalia
     Tel: +86 (0)10 8511 2958   Tel: +852 2375 4001

American Airlines
     Tel: 400-886-1001 (*within China*)
     Tel: +852 3678 8500

All Nippon Airways
     Tel: +86 (0)10 6590 9191   Tel: +852 2810 7100

Asiana Airlines   Tel: 400 650 8000
(Within China)   Tel: +852 2523 8585

Austrian Airlines
     Tel: +86 (0)10 6464 5999   Tel: +852 2525 5221

Bangkok Airways   Tel: +852 2899 2597

Bangladesh BIMAN   Tel: +852 2724 8600

British Airways
     Tel: +86 (0)10 6459 0081   Tel: +852 2822 9000

Cathay Pacific
     Tel: +86 (0)10 6459 0038   Tel: +852 2747 1888

China Airlines
     Tel: +86 (0)10 6510 2671   Tel:+852 2843 9800

China Eastern Airlines
     Tel: +852 2861 0288

Delta Airlines
     Tel: +86 (0)10 5879 7468   Tel: +852 2620 6678

A1

EgyptAir
    Tel: +86 (0)10 8527 5000

EL AL Israel
    Tel: +86 (0)10 5879 7358   Tel: +852 2380 3362

Emirates Airlines
    Tel: +86 (0)10 5108 8696   Tel: +852 2801 8777

Ethiopian Airlines
    Tel: +86 (0)10 6505 0314   Tel: +852 2117 0233

EVA Airways
    Tel: +86 (0)10 6563 5000   Tel: +852 2810 9251

Finnair Tel: +86 (0)10 6512 7180   Tel: +852 2117 1238

Garuda Indonesia
    Tel: +86 (0)10 5879 0984   Tel: +852 2522 9140

Japan Airlines
    Tel: 4008 88 0808 (*within China*)
    Tel: +852 2523 0081

Jet Airways   Tel: +852 2523 7762

Kenya Airways   Tel: +852 3678 2000

KLM   Tel: 4008 808 222 (*within China*)
    Tel: +852 2808 2168

Korean Airlines
    Tel: +86 (0)10 8453 8421   Tel: 852 2733 7110

Lufthansa
    Tel: +86 (0)10 6468 8838   Tel: +852 2868 2313

Malaysia Airlines
    Tel: +86 (0)10 6505 0341   Tel: +852 2916 0088

Northwest Airlines
    Tel: 40081 40081(*within China*)

MIAT Mongolian
    Tel: +86 (0)10 650 79297

Oasis Hong Kong Airlines
    Tel: +852 3628 0628

Orient Thai Airways
    Tel: +852 2366 5869

Philippines Airlines
    Tel: +86 (0)10 6510 2991

PIA- Pakistan Inter.
    Tel: +86 (0)10 6505 1681   Tel: +852 2366 4770

A1

Qantas Tel: +86 (0)10 6567 9006   Tel: +852 2822 9000

Qatar Airways
        Tel: +86 (0)10 5923 5100   Tel: +852 2868 9833

Royal Brunei Airlines
        Tel: +852 2747 1888

Royal Nepal Airlines
        Tel: +852 2375 2180

SAS Scandinavian
        Tel: +852 2865 1370

Singapore Airlines
        Tel: +86 (0)10 6505 2233   Tel: +852 2520 2233

South African Airways
        Tel: +852 2722 5768

Sri Lankan Airlines
        Tel: +86 (0)10 6461 7208   Tel: +852 2521 0812

Swissair
        Tel: +86 (0)10 8454 0180   Tel: +852 3002 1330

Thai Airways
        Tel: +86 (0)10 8515 0088   Tel: +852 2876 6899

Turkish Airlines
        Tel: +86 (0)10 6465 1867   Tel: +852 3101 0592

United Airlines
        Tel: +86 (0)10 8468 6666   Tel: +852 2810 4888

Uzbekistan Airways
        Tel: +86 (0)10 6500 6442

Vietnam Airlines
        Tel: +86 (0)10 8454 1196   Tel: +852 2810 6680

Virgin Atlantic Airways
        Tel: +852 2532 3081

Hotels

It's not possible to list all the hotels in China. A full list of
hotels on the mainland, Hong Kong and Macau is available
on: www.chinaetravel.com and www.hongkonghotels.com.

Beijing

Beijing Hotel *****
33 East Changan Avenue
Tel: +86 (0)10 65137766
Website: www.chinabeijinghotel.com

A1

Kempinski Hotel Beijing Lufthansa Center *****
50 Liangmaqiao Road
Tel: +86 (0)10 64653388;
Website: www.kempinski-beijing.com

Shangri-La Hotel *****
29 Zizhuyuan Road
Tel: +86 (0)10 68412211;
Website: www.shangri-la.com

Sheraton Great Wall Hotel *****
10 North Dongsanhuan Road
Tel: +86 (0)10 65905566;
Website: www.sheraton.com/greatwall

Kunkun Hotel *****
2 South Xinyuan Road
Tel: +86 (0)10 65903388;
Website: www.hotelkunlun.com

Holiday Inn Lido ****
Jiangtai Road & Jichang Road
Tel: +86 (0)10 64376688

Wangfujing Grand Hotel ****
57 Wangfujing Avenue
Tel: +86 (0)10 65221188/65138912;
Website: www.wangfujinghotel.com

Beijing Grand Skylight Hotel ***
45A North Xinhua Street
Tel: +86 (0)10) 66071166

21st Century Hotel Beijing ***
40 Liangmaqiao Road
Tel: +86 (0)10 64663311

Dalian

Best Western Premier Dalian Harbour View Hotel *****
2 Gangwan Street Zhongshan District
Tel: +86 (0)411 8272 8888;
Website: www.bestwestern.com

Furama Hotel Dalian *****
60 Renmin Road
Tel: +86 (0)411 2630888;
Website: www.furama.com.cn

Holiday Inn Dalian ✳✳✳✳
No. 189 Tianjin Street
Tel: +86 (0)411 88138888;
E-mail: hotel@expresshidl.com

Gloria Plaza Hotel ✳✳✳✳
5 Yide Street
Tel: +86 (0)411 2808855;
Website: www.gphdalian.com

Sea Horizon Hotel Dalian ✳✳✳✳
81 West Haibin Road
Tel: +86 (0)411 2403399;
Website: www.seahorizon-hotel.com.cn

Wanda International Hotel ✳✳✳
539 Changjiang Road
Tel: +86 (0)411 3628888;
Website: www.wdih.com

Grand Hotel Dalian ✳✳✳
1 Jiefang Street
Tel: +86 (0)411 2806161

Guangzhou

White Swan ✳✳✳✳✳
1 South Shamian Street
Tel: +86 (0)20 81886968;
Website: www.white-swan-hotel.com

The Garden Hotel ✳✳✳✳✳
368 Huanshi Dong Lu
Tel: +82 (0)20 83338989;
Website: www.gardenhotel-guangzhou.com

Marriott China Hotel ✳✳✳✳✳
Liuhua Road
Tel: +86 (0)20 86666888

Guangdong International Hotel ✳✳✳✳✳
339 Huanshi Dong Road
Tel: +86 (0)20 83311888

Dongfang Hotel ✳✳✳✳
120 Liuhua Road
Tel: +86 (0)20 86669900

Bai Yun Hotel ✳✳✳✳
367 East Huanshi Road
Tel: +86 (0)20 83333998;
Website: www.baiyun-hotel.com

A1

Ocean Hotel ***
412 East Huanshi Road
Tel: +86 (0)20 87765988

Guangzhou Hotel ***
Haizhu Square
Tel: +86 (0)20 83338168

Hong Kong

Conrad International Hotel *****
Pacific Place, 88 Queensway
Tel: +852 25213838;
Website: www.conrad.com.hk

Excelsior *****
281 Gloucester Road, Causeway Bay
Tel: +852 28948888;
Website: www.mandarin-oriental.com

Hotel Nikko *****
72 Mody Road, Tsim Sha Tsui East
Tel: +852 27391111;
Website: www.hotelnikko.com.hk

Century Harbour Hotel Hong Kong *****
508 Queen's Road
Tel: +852 29741234;
Website: www.century-harbour-hotel.com

Renaissance Harbour View ****
1 Harbour Road
Tel: +852 28028888;
Website: www.renaissancehotels.com/hkghv

Holiday Inn Golden Mile ****
50 Nathan Road, Tsim Sha Tsui
Tel: +852 23693111;
Website: www.goldenmile.com

Wharney Hotel ***
57-73 Lockhart Road, Wan Chai
Tel: +852 28611000

Newton Hotel Hong Kong ***
218 Electric Road, North Point, Hong Kong
Tel: +852 28072333;
Website: www.newtonhk.com

A1

Shanghai

Jinjiang Tower Hotel *****
161 Changle Road
Tel: +86 (0)21 64151188;
Website: www.jjtcn.com

The Westin Tai Ping Yang *****
5 South Zunyi Road
Tel: +86 (0)21 62758888;
Website: www.westin-shanghai.com

Grand Hyatt Shanghai *****
Jin Mao Tower, 2 Century Boulevard
Tel: +86 (0)21 50491234;
Website: http://shanghai.hyatt.com/hyatt/

The Portman Ritz Carlton Shanghai *****
1376 West Nanjing Road
Tel: +86 (0)21 62798888;
Website: www.ritz-carlton.com

Jinjiang Hotel ****
59 South Maoming Road
Tel: +86 (0)21 62582582

Crowne Plaza Shanghai ****
400 Panyu Road
Tel: +86 (0)21 62808888;
Website: www.crowneplaza.com.cn

Radisson SAS Lansheng Hotel ****
1000 Quyang Road
Tel: +86 (0)21 65428000;
Website: www.radisson.com

Rainbow Hotel, Shanghai ****
2000 Yanan West Road
Tel: +86 (0)21 62753388/62752640;
Website: www.rainbowhotel.net

Yangtze New World Shanghai ****
2099 West Yan'an Road
Tel: +86 (0)21 62750000

Pacific Hotel ***
108 West Nanjing Road
Tel: +86 (0)21 63276226

A1

Shenzhen

Panglin Hilton Hotel *****
2002 Jiabin Road
Tel: +86 (0)755 2518 5888;
Website: www.panglin-hotel.com

Landmark Hotel *****
3018 Nanhu Road
Tel: +86 (0)755 2172288

Shangri-La Shenzhen *****
East Side Railway Station, Jianshe Road
Tel: +86 (0)755 2330888;
Website: www.shangri-la.com

Nanhai Hotel *****
1 Shekou Industrial Estate
Tel: +86 (0)755 6692888;
Website: www.nanhai-hotel.com

Nanshan Donghua Holiday Inn ****
Donghua Gongyuan
Tel: +86 (0)755 6416688

Hotel Orient Region ****
Shennan Zhong Road
Tel: +86 (0)755 2247000

Useful websites in China

www.made-in-china.com – For importers and exporters, and trade show information.

www.gov.cn – The Official Chinese Central Government Website

www.alibaba.com – Trade directory for import/export to/from China

www.asiaexpat.com – Expat website

www.yp.com.cn/english – China Yellow Pages Website

www.fmprc.gov.cn/eng – Ministry of Foreign Affairs of the People's Republic of China

www.chinaeconomicreview.com – Website for up to date economic information on China

www.dgmarket.com – Online trade magazine

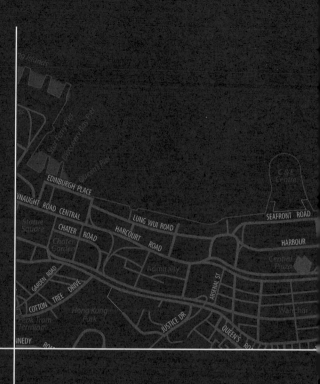

appendix two

appendix two

Chinese Language

It has already been mentioned that in China there is one common written language but a vast number of dialects.

The national language is Mandarin (Putonghua) which is based on the Beijing dialect, whereas in the south of China and Hong Kong, Cantonese is widely spoken. A person from Hong Kong or Guangzhou would have difficulty communicating orally with someone from Beijing although they could write to each other.

There is, however, a form of standard Chinese, based on the pronunciation of the northern dialects, and in particular, the Beijing dialect. This is referrred to as Pinyin and is basically the phonetic transcription of the language of the Han people.

It is perhaps reassuring to the visitor to learn that English is increasingly being used in China, but it is useful to know a few familiar phrases, your Chinese colleagues will be flattered and impressed, and you will know if they are talking about you.

Putonghua has four tones, spoken with emphasis. The first tone is high and level, the second starting low and rising, the third falling and then rising, and the fourth falling. However, there are some variations in the tones, and it really depends on the dialect, intonation and education of the natural speaker.

A2

Useful Phrases

Pinyin Alphabet

a (a)   Vowel as in *far*
b (p)   Consonant as in *be*
c (ts') Consonant as in *chip*; strongly aspirated
d (t)   Consonant as in *do*
e (e)   Vowel as in *her*
f (f)   Consonant as in *foot*
g (k') Consonant as in *go*
h (h)   Consonant as in *her*; strongly aspirated
i (i)   Vowel as in *eat* or as in *sir* (when in syllables beginning with c, ch, r, s, sh, z and zh.)
j (ch) Consonant as in *jeep*
k (k') Consonant as in *kind*, strongly aspirated
l (l)   Consonant as in *land*
m (m) Consonant as in *me*
n (n)   Consonant as in *now*

o (o)   Vowel as in *law*

p (p')   Consonant as in *par*; strongly aspirated

q (ch')   Consonant as in *cheek*

r (j)   Consonant as in *right*; (not rolled) or pronounced as *z* in *azure*

s (s, ss, sz)   Consonant as in *sister*

sh (sh)   Consonant as in *shore*

t (t')   Consonant as in *top*; strongly aspirated

u (u)   Vowel as in *too*; also as in French *tu* or the German München

v (v)   Consonant used only to produce foreign words, national minority words, and local dialects

w (w)   Semi-vowel in syllables beginning with u when not preceded by a consonant, as in *want*

x (hs)   Consonant as in *she*

y   Semi-vowel in syllables beginning with i or u when not preceded by a consonant, as in *yet*

z (ts, tz)   Consonant as in *adze*

zh (ch)   Consonant as in *jump*

I, me; mine	wô (*waw*); wôde (*wah-duh*)
You; your	nî (*nee*); nîde (*nee-duh*)
He, it/she	tä (*tah*) / tä (*tah*)
His, its/hers	täde (*tah-duh*) / täde (*tah-duh*)
We, us	wômen (*waw-mun*)
You (pl.)	nîmen (*nee-mun*)
They, them (m./f.)	tämen (*tah-mun*) / tämen (*tah-mun*)
Their (m./f.)	tämende (*tah-mun-duh*) / tämende (*tah-mun-duh*)

Hello, how are you?
nî hâo; (*nee hao*); nî hâo ma (*nee hao mah*

Good morning	zâo (*dzao*); zâo än (*dzao an*)
Good evening	wân än (*wahn an*)
Good-bye	zaì jiàn (*dzai jee-en*)

I don't understand wô bù dông (*waw boo doong*)

Yes, I agree; correct
shì (*shir*); dùi (*doo-ay*)

I don't agree	bù tóngyì (*boo toong-yee*)
Please	qîng (*ching*)

Thank you; many thanks
xiè xie (*shee-eh shee-eh*); düo xiè (*dwaw shee-eh*)

It's nothing (don't mention it)
bú kèqì (*boo kuh-chee*)

I'm sorry   duì bùqî (*doo-ay boo chee*)

A2

OK, you can	kêyî (*kuh-ee*)
Not OK, you can't	bú kêyî (*boo kuh-ee*)
Not bad, so-so	hái kêyî (*hi kuh-ee*)
Good; very good	hâo (*hao*); hên hâo (*hun hao*)
No (not) good	bù hâo (*boo hao*)
Thank you but I...	xiè xie, wô... (*she-eh, waw...*)
am unable to	bù néng (*boo nung*)
don't want to	bú yào (*boo yao*)
don't like	bù xîhuän (*boo shee-hwahn*
Pleased; happy	huänxî (*hwahn-shee*)
Very; extremely	hên (*hun*); fëicháng (*fay-chahng*)
Slow	màn (*man*)
Fast	kuài (*kwhy*)
Hot	rè (*ruh*)
Cold	lêng (*lung*)
Who?	shúi (*shway*)
When is...?	shénma shíhòu (*shum-mah shir-hoe*)
Where...;...is where...?	shénma dìfang... (*shum-mah dee fahng...*); ...zài nâlî (*...dzai nah-lee*)
Friend péngyôu	(*pung-yo*)
Friendly	yôu hâo (*yo-hao*)
May I please ask your name?	
	qîngwèn guìxìng (*ching-win gway-shing*)
My name is...	wô jiaò (*waw djeeow*)
I am	wio shì (*waw shir*)
American	mêiguórén (*may-gwaw run*)
Australian	àudàlìyârén (*ow-dah-lee-ah run*)
British	yïnggúorén (*ying-gwaw run*)
Canadian	jiänadaren (*jee-ah-nah-dah run*)

Travel

Right	yòu (*yo*)
Left	zûo (*dzwaw*)
Front	qián (*chee-en*)
Back	hòu (*hoe*)
Luggage	xínglî (*shing-lee*)
Customs	hâiguän (*hye-gwan*)
Car	qìchë (*chee-chuh*)
Bus	gönggòng qìchë (gung-gung *cheecheh*)
Taxi	chüzü qìchë (*choo-dzoo chee-cheh*)
Airport	fëijïchâng (*fay-jee-chahng*)
Railway station	huôchëzhàn (*hwaw-cheh jan*)
Bicycle	zìxíngchë (*dze-sing-cheh*)
Bicycle rental	chüzü zìxíngchë (*choo-dzoo-dze-sing-cheh*)

A2

At the Hotel

Hotel	lûguân (*lu-gwan*)
Room	fángjiän (*fahng-jee-en*)
Key	yàoshi (*yao shir*)
Floor	lóu (*lo*)
Lift (elevator)	diàntï (*dee-en tee*)
Stairs	lóutï (*low-tee*)
Telephone	diànhuà (*dee-en-hwa*)
Light (electric)	diàndëng (*dee-endung*)
Fridge	bïng xiäng (*bing-shee-ahng*)
Television	diàn shì (*dee-en-shr*)
Radio	shöuyïnjï (*show-yin-gee*)
Air-conditioning	köngtiáo/lêngqì (*kawng-tyaw/lung-chee*)
Laundry	xîyïdian (*shee yee dee-en*)
Toilet	cèsuô (*tse-swo*)
Men's	nán (*nahn*)
Women's	nû (*new*)
Bath	xîzâo (*shee-dzao*)
Water	shûi (*shway*)
Please come in	qîng jinlai (*ching jeen-lye*)
(Please) wait a moment	dêngyïdeng (*dung-yee-dung*)
Sleep	shùizháo (*shway-jao*)
Bed	chuáng (*chew-ahng*)
Sheets	chuáng dän (*chew-ahng don*)
Towel	maó jïn (*mao jeen*)
Clean	gän jìng (*gahn jeeng*)
Not clean	bù gän jìng (*boo gahn jeeng*)
Have	yôu (*yo*)
Not have	méi yôu (*may yo*)
Hotel restaurant	cän tïng (*kahn teeng*)
Hotel shop	xiâomàibù (*shao my boo*)
Post office	yóujú (*yo-joo*)
barber shop	lîfâdìan (*lee-fah-dee-en*)

Sightseeing

Welcome	huänyîng (*hwahn-ying*)
We would like to visit a...	wômen yào qù... (*waw-mun yao chu*)
See, watch	kàn (*kahn*)
Factory	göngchâng (*goong chahng*)
Museum	bówùguân (*baw-woo-gwan*)
Park	göngyuán (*goong-yoo-ahn*)
School	xuéxiào (*shoo-eh shee-ow*)
Shop	shängdiàn (*shahng-dee-en*)

University	dàxué (*da shoo-eh*)
Temple	sìmiào (*suh-myao*)
Buddhist temple	sì (*see*)
Confucian temple	miào (*mee-yao*)
Daoist temple	guàn (*gwahn*)
Take a picture	zhàoxiàng (*jao shee-ahng*)

Shopping

Antique	gûdông (*goo-doong*)
Artworks	yìshùpîn (*ee-shoo-peen*)
Book	shü (*shoo*)
Bookshop	shüdiàn (*shoo dee-en*)
Department store	bâihuòshängdiàn (*bye-hwaw shahng-dee-en*)
Handicrafts; art	göngyìpîn (*goong yee-peen*)
Stamps	yóupiaò (*yo-pee-ow*)
How much (money)?	
	duöshâo qián (*dwaw-shao chee-en*)
Expensive	gùi (*gway*)
Cheap	piányi (*pee-en yee*)
Change	língqián (*leeng-chh-en*)
Where can I buy...?	
	zài nâlî kêyî mâi (*dzai nah-lee kuh-yee my*)
I would like that...	wô yào nèige... (*waw-yao nay-guh...*)
black one	hëide (*hay-duh*)
blue one	lánde (*lahn-duh*)
green one	lùde (*lee-yu-duh*)
red one	hóngde (*hoong-duh*)
white one	báide (*bye-duh*)
yellow one	huângde (*hoo-ahng-duh*)
brown one	zöngde (*dzong-de*)
grey one	hüide (*hoo-ay-duh*)

A2

Food

I am hungry	wô èle (*waw uh-luh*)
I am thirsty	wô kële (*waw kuh-luh*)
Eat	chï (*chir*)
Drink	hë (*huh*)
Restaurant	fànguân (*fahn gwan*)
Breakfast	zâocän (*dzao-tsahn*)
	zâofàn (*dzao-fan*)
Lunch	wûcän (*woo-tsahn*)
	wûfän (*woo-fan*)
Dinner	wâncän (*wahn-tsahn*)
	wânfàn (*wahn-fan*)

Snack/dessert	diânxïn (*dee-en sheen*)
Chopsticks	kuàizi (*kwhy-dzih*)
Knife	däo (*dao*)
Fork	chä (*chah*)
Spoon	tängchi (*tahng-chir*)
What is your speciality?	
	yôu shénma tèbiéde hâochi
	(*yo shummahtuh-bee-eh-duh*
	hao-chir)
I've had enough to eat	
	chïbâole (*chir-bao-luh*)
The food was delicious	
	hên hâochï (*hun hao-chir*)
Cheers!	gänbëi (*gahn-bei*)
Water (cold)	liángkäishûi (*lee-ahng kai-shway*)
Coffee	käfëi (*kah-fay*)
Tea	chà (*chah*)
Beer	píjiû (*pee-jee-oh*)
Beef	niúròu (*nee-oh row*)
Chicken	jï (*jee*)
Duck	yäzi (*yah-dzih*)
Pork	zhüroù (*jew-ro*)
Fish	yú (*yu*)
Shrimp	xiä (*shee-yah*)
Eggs	jïdàn (*jee-dan*)
Rice	fàn (*fahn*)
Vegetables	qïngcài (*ching-tsye*)
Soup	täng (*tahng*)
Fruit	shûiguô (*shway-gwaw*)
Apple	píngguô (*ping-gwaw*)
Banana	xiängjiäo (*shee-ahng-je-ow*)
Orange	júzi (*ju-dzih*)
Peach	táozi (*tao-dzih*)
Pear	lízi (*lee-dzih*)
Watermelon	xïguä (*shee-gwa*)
Ice-cream	bïngqílín (*bing-chee-leen*)
Western food	xïcän (*shee-tsahn*)
Vegetarian	chïsù (*chir soo*)
Sweet	tián (*tee-en*)
Sour	suän (*swan*)
Bitter	kû (*koo*)
Spicy (hot)	là (*lah*)

Health care/Medicine

Medicine	yào (*yao*)
Pharmacy	yàodiàn (*yao deen-en*)

A2

Where can I find medicine?

    nâlî yôu yào mâi (*nah-lee yo yao my*)

Aspirin   **äsïpîlín (ah-suh-pee-leen)**

I have a cold   wô gônmàole (*waw gone-mao-luh*)

I don't feel well   wô bù shüfu (*waw boo shoo-foo*)

I am ill   wô bìngle (*waw beeng-luh*)

Call a doctor   qîng yïshëng lái (*ching yee-shung lye*)

Dentist   yáyï (*yah-yee*)

Hospital   yïyuàn (*yee yoo-en*)

Headache   tóutòng (*toe-tuhng*)

Toothache   yátòng (*yah-tuhng*)

Dizziness   tóuyùn (*toe yew-win*)

Diarrhoea   lädùzi (*lah doo-dzi*)

Stomach sickness   wèibìng (*way-bing*)

Stomach pain   wèitòng (*way-tuhng*)

It hurts me here   wô zhèli tòng (*waw juh-lee tuhng*)

Time

What time is it?   jîdîan zhong (*jee dee-en joong*)

[number] o'clock   ...dian zhöng (*...dee-en joong*)

Morning   zâoshàng (*dzao-shahng*)

Midday   zhöngwû (*joong-woo*)

Evening   wânshàng (*wahn-shahng*)

Yesterday   zuótiän (*dzwaw-tee-en*)

Today   jïntiän (*jeen-tee-en*)

Tomorrow   míngtiän (*ming-tee-en*)

Day   tiän (*tee-en*)

Month   yuè (*yweh*)

Year   nián (*nee-en*)

A2

Numbers

One   yï (*yee*)

Two   èr (*are*)

Three   sän (*san*)

Four   sì (*suh*)

Five   wû (*woo*)

Six   liù (*lee-oh*)

Seven   qï (*chee*)

Eight   bä (*bah*)

Nine   jiû (*jee-oh*)

Ten   shí (*shir*)

Eleven   shíyï (*shir-yee*)

Twelve   shîèr (*shir-yee*)

Thirteen   shísän (*shir-san*)

Fourteen   shísì (*shir-suh*)

Twenty	èrshí (*are-shir*)
Thirty	sänshí (*san-shir*)
One hundred	yïbâi (*yee-bye*)
One thousand	yïqiän (*yee-chee-en*)

A2